"Paul Tripp writes out of the experience of his own suffering and his skill as a pastor/counselor in helping people through times of trouble. He knows what it is like to go through the storms of life, but more importantly, he knows where to find shelter. This book will help anyone who is hoping to find refuge."

—Philip Ryken, Senior Minister, Tenth Presbyterian Church, Philadelphia

"Can one psalm really change your life? It can if you dig deeply enough. *A Shelter in the Time of Storm* is Paul Tripp at his finest—excavating Psalm 27 with clarity, potency, and straight-to-the-heart relevance. When troubles come knocking, do yourself a favor: let this book teach you how to treasure no less than 52 life-transforming truths from this grace-filled psalm."

—Dave Harvey, church care and church planting, Sovereign Grace Ministries; author, *When Sinners Say "I Do."*

a SHELTER in the time OF STORM

meditations on God and trouble

PAUL DAVID TRIPP

WHEATON, ILLINOIS

Malcolm,
You have known me for many years,
yet you have remained my friend.
Thank you.

A Shelter in the Time of Storm: Meditations on God and Trouble

Published by Crossway
1300 Crescent Street
Wheaton, Illinois 60187

Cover design: Jon McGrath

Cover photo: Veer

First printing 2009

Printed in the United States of America

PDF ISBN: 978-1-4335-0599-7

Mobipocket ISBN: 978-1-4335-0600-0

Library of Congress Cataloging-in-Publication Data

Tripp, Paul David, 1950–
A shelter in the time of storm : meditations on God and trouble / Paul David Tripp.
p. cm.
ISBN 978-1-4335-0598-0 (tpb)
1. Bible. O.T. Psalms XXVII—Meditations. I. Title.
BS145027th.T75 2009
223'.206—dc22 2008044152

Crossway is a publishing ministry of Good News Publishers.

VP 19 18 17 16 15 14 13
15 14 13 12 11 10 9 8 7 6

Contents

Introduction: Hope in God in a World That Is Broken

It was the call no parent ever wants to get. Our daughter had been walking down the street in Philadelphia when a drunk and unlicensed driver careened onto the sidewalk and crushed her against a wall. It was the beginning of many, many months of travail. (By God's grace she is doing very well now.)

There are many mysteries to this moment in our lives that we will never solve. Yet, there are a few things that we know for sure. We really do live in a fallen world. We haven't been given a ticket out of the brokenness of this world simply because we are the children of God. What happened to our daughter was a horrible injustice, followed by day upon day of remarkable pain. The world we live in simply is not operating the way God intended.

There is a second thing we know for sure. There is a God of awesome grace who meets his children in moments of darkness and difficulty. He is worth running to. He is worth waiting for. He brings rest when it seems like there is no rest to be found.

But there is a third thing. You and I were just not hardwired to make our way through this fallen world on our own. We were meant to exist with eyes filled with the beauty of his presence and hearts at rest in the lap of his goodness. This is what I love about the Psalms. They put difficulty and hope together in the tension of hardship and grace that is the life of everyone this side of eternity.

It is not hard to recognize the environment of the Psalms. The Psalms live in your city, on your street, in your family. The Psalms tell your story. It is a story of hope and disappointment, of need and provision, of fear and mystery, of struggle and rest, and of God's boundless love and amazing grace. People in the psalms get angry, grow afraid, cry out in confusion, survive opposition, hope for better days, hurt one another, help one another, run from God, trust in God, make foolish choices, ask for forgiveness, and grow wiser and stronger. They are people just like you and me.

Psalm 27 is a psalm of honesty and hope. Like real life, it is written between the tension of a life of trouble and a God of grace. It is a psalm of fear, but in it fear gives way to confidence. It is a psalm of danger, but it speaks with power and practicality of the safety that can be found in the Lord. In many ways it is a sad psalm, yet it is punctuated with songs of joy. It is a psalm of rejection, but it sings the acceptance of the Lord. It is a psalm of action, yet it finds its strength in waiting on the Lord. There are four things that draw me to this psalm.

1) *Its shock value.* David is writing about being under attack. The words are graphic and clear: "When evildoers assail me to eat up my flesh, my adversaries and foes. . . . Though an army encamp against me . . . though war arise against me. . . . For false witnesses have risen against me, and they breathe out violence."

These would be difficult circumstances for any of us, but think with me: if you were in the middle of them, what is the first thing you would pray for? What is the central thing you would desire? You almost can't help but be shocked by David's response. He doesn't crave vengeance. He doesn't cry out first for protection or justice. No, David's first thoughts run to the temple, where the Lord dwells. The first desire of his heart is to gaze upon the beauty of the Lord. At first look, this response seems almost shockingly unnatural, that is, until you let Psalm 27 teach you about faith, safety, and the presence of the Lord.

2) *Its regularity.* For all of its seeming shock value, Psalm 27 gives an accurate and familiar picture of what normal life is like in a fallen world. A moment of high worship is followed by a situation of trouble. A moment of insight is followed by a moment of confusion. Rest is followed by threat. Call to action is followed by the need to wait. Confidence that God is near is followed by a desperate plea that he would hear and answer. These are the variegated colors of a world in need of restoration. These are the regular ups and downs, ins and outs, and highs and lows of living with the Lord in a place

that is broken. When you read this psalm, you get the impression that David lived where we live.

3) *Its focus on Christ.* Underneath the psalm's accurate depiction of the here-and-there experiences of the world we all live in is a deeper theme. This theme is really the unifying theme of the psalm. It is the thing that gives this psalm of trouble and faith its hope. What is this theme? It is Christ. All of the fingers of this psalm point to Christ. Jesus came to earth, knowing the trouble he would face, but he was not afraid; he knew his Father would be his light and salvation. Jesus knew that his enemies would stumble and fall.

In the cross's most dramatic moment, it was Jesus who cried for his Father not to turn away in anger. It was Jesus who said he would not be alone, even though his father and mother would forsake him. Jesus faced the false witnesses who were intent on violence. Beneath everything else, this is a psalm of sin and redemption, and because of that, again and again it points us to the Redeemer who will come to suffer injustice, violence, and ultimately the rejection of his Father so that we might know forgiveness, acceptance, life, and hope.

4) *Its call to patient hope.* This is not a cynical, survivalist psalm. It does not have an "I've been taken once and it won't happen again" feel to it. For all of the trouble that courses its way through this psalm, it is in the end a psalm of bright and lasting hope. It doesn't call us to live self-protectively. It doesn't give us seven steps for avoiding the difficulties of the fallen world.

No, Psalm 27 tells that even in the middle of difficulties that we do not understand nor seem able to escape, we have reason to take heart and have hope. And the hope of Psalm 27 is not like the hope of a child who has just been promised ice cream in a few hours. The child *does* hope that the ice cream will actually materialize, and she believes it will because she believes that her parents really love her. But she will come back every five minutes to ask you if it's time for ice cream yet! The hope of Psalm 27 is patient, and it grows stronger as it waits, because it is rooted in a daily consideration of the goodness of the Lord.

This really does speak into the familiar realities of your life and mine with challenge and hope, with conviction and encouragement, and with honesty and the gospel of the Lord Jesus Christ.

Let me say a little bit about the fifty-two meditations that you will be reading. You are not holding an exegetical commentary on Psalm 27. I have approached the psalm like a wood butcher. The wood butcher cuts into a log, looking for boards with a particularly interesting or elegant grain, and cuts them out like a meat butcher would do with a fine steak. Then he places them next to other boards of similar beauty and assembles them into a table, a chair, or a fine wooden box. He assembles the pieces intentionally to help others see their individual and collective beauty in a way they wouldn't without his eyes and his hands.

I have cut into the log of Psalm 27 and pulled out themes of interesting and elegant grain and assembled them into a picture of how to live with hope in God in a world that is fallen. No two of these reflections are exactly alike. Each has a different grain, yet each is meant to catch your attention and help you to see. My hope is that as you examine the variegated grains of truth that are in this psalm, you will not settle for self-protection or survival. My hope is that these reflections will fill your heart with a patient hope that grows stronger as the trouble-spotted days go by.

Psalm 27 and Everyday Life

Psalm 27 really is an amazing psalm. There are moments when it soars with the thoughts of what it means to be a child of the Lord. There are places where it reaches into the harshest realities of life in a very broken world. There are times when this psalm is a scalpel, cutting through the layers and exposing the heart. It is a psalm of worship, commitment, trouble, beauty, and patience. There is a way in which Psalm 27 is like a biblical worldview presented as a podcast. There simply is much more there than you think there is after your first reading.

I had a friend who had quite a large rose garden. He was very dedicated to doing all the daily tasks necessary to keep his roses healthy. But it hit him one day that he'd taken no time to actually enjoy the roses that he was so zealous to tend. So one afternoon he did just that. He sat down in front of one of his rose bushes for three hours. As he sat, he began to see, smell, and hear things that he wouldn't have experienced any other way. Contrary to what you may think, the time didn't drag on. He was enthralled by the created glory that he was taking in. And as he sat there, he began to realize why those bushes were worth the commitment and the effort that he'd been investing.

But there's more. After his three-hour gaze of that one bush, he would never—could never—look at roses as he once did. That afternoon he saw, really saw, what a rose was about, and new sight changed him. So, I'm inviting you to sit down with me in front of Psalm 27. I'm inviting you to keep your eyes focused and your ears tuned. I'm inviting you to open your heart to what you may have been too busy to see. I'm inviting you to gaze upon the beauty of the Lord. And I would imagine that if you are willing to do that, like my friend, somehow, someway, you'll get up a changed person.

Paul David Tripp
March 6, 2008

Psalm 27

The Lord is my light and my salvation;
  whom shall I fear?
The Lord is the stronghold of my life;
  of whom shall I be afraid?

When evildoers assail me
  to eat up my flesh,
my adversaries and foes,
  it is they who stumble and fall.

Though an army encamp against me,
  my heart shall not fear;
though war arise against me,
  yet I will be confident.

One thing have I asked of the Lord,
  that will I seek after:
that I may dwell in the house of the Lord
  all the days of my life,
to gaze upon the beauty of the Lord
  and to inquire in his temple.

For he will hide me in his shelter
  in the day of trouble;
he will conceal me under the cover of his tent;
  he will lift me high upon a rock.

And now my head shall be lifted up
  above my enemies all around me,
and I will offer in his tent
  sacrifices with shouts of joy;
I will sing and make melody to the Lord.

Hear, O Lord, when I cry aloud;
  be gracious to me and answer me!
You have said, "Seek my face."
My heart says to you,
  "Your face, Lord, do I seek."
  Hide not your face from me.

Turn not your servant away in anger,
O you who have been my help.
Cast me not off; forsake me not,
O God of my salvation!
For my father and my mother have forsaken me,
but the Lord will take me in.

Teach me your way, O Lord,
and lead me on a level path
because of my enemies.
Give me not up to the will of my adversaries;
for false witnesses have risen against me,
and they breathe out violence.

I believe that I shall look upon the goodness of the Lord
in the land of the living!
Wait for the Lord;
be strong, and let your heart take courage;
wait for the Lord!

Meditations

1 | Life as a Student

> Teach me your way, O LORD,
> and lead me on a level path
> because of my enemies.
>
> PSALM 27:11

Do you think that you've arrived? Do you tend to think that you've learned what you need to learn and now know what you need to know? Do you see yourself as having more answers than questions? Do your carry around a hunger to know? Do you want to understand more deeply and more fully? Do you have a humble, open, and seeking heart? Are you approaching life with the mentality of a student?

Here is a prayer to be taught. Do you pray this? How often? I think there's much pride of knowing and the accompanying mental lethargy in many of us. There was a time, in the early years of our faith, when we couldn't get enough. We had a voracious hunger for truth and a lively fear of falsehood. We lived with the humbling realization that there was so much that we didn't know. We loved walking through the gallery of God's wisdom, taking in the treasures there. We loved listening to fellow students who were further along the path of wisdom than we. We loved to be pointed to nuggets of wisdom that could have come only from the mouth of the Divine. We loved to study the Word of God, to examine each phrase, comparing Scripture with Scripture. We could not get enough, we were not satisfied; we were students.

But something happened along the way. Perhaps we got distracted by the physical pleasures of the created world and began to live more like tourists than students. Perhaps we got discouraged by the troubles of the world and felt our study was not helping us. Maybe we got sidetracked by our own purposes and plans and had little time left to be students. Or perhaps our hunger was blunted by assessments of arrival. Perhaps we came to think that we knew all that we needed to know.

Yet, there are two reasons that remain to pray this prayer: depth and danger. Why would I pray to be taught again and again and again by the Lord? Because his wisdom is just that deep and vast. His wisdom has no boundary. His wisdom has no bottom. His wisdom has no ceiling. If for ten million years I would sit for twenty-four hours a day at his feet and listen, I would scratch only the very surface of the wisdom that is his. If I gave every day of my life to study only the wisdom that is captured on the pages of Scripture, I could study until my very last day and not have mined all the treasures of wisdom that are there. So, once more, I pray to be taught because the wisdom of God is just that deep.

I also pray this prayer because I live in a world of danger. It's a world where the sounds of falsehood echo more loudly and repeatedly than the sounds of wisdom. Living in human culture is like sitting in a twenty-thousand-seat arena just before the concert begins. Everyone is talking at once, a den of voices so loud and pervasive you can barely hear yourself think. Every day a thousand voices speak into my life and the vast majority of those voices have not gotten the flowers of their insight from the wisdom garden of the Lord.

They tell me who I am. They tell me what life is about. They tell me how to invest my time. They tell me how to use my resources. They tell me how to conduct my relationships. They tell me what is true and untrue. They tell me what my goals should be. They tell me what the good life looks like. They tell me what I should be and do and want. They offer me a comprehensive system of wisdom that's well thought through and attractive on many levels, but that competes with the true wisdom that can come only from God. It's so easy to be taken captive. It's so easy to have divine wisdom corrupted by human wisdom. It's so easy to breathe in the polluted air of a culture that no longer actually thinks that God is, let alone that he is wise.

So, with a lively acknowledgment of the vastness of the depth of God's wisdom and a healthy fear of the germs of falsehood that are everywhere around me, I accept the fact that on this side of eternity I live in the middle of a raging wisdom war. So, I pray for the strength, protection, direction, and encouragement that can only be found when I am a student of the Lord. Morning after morning I bow my head and humbly pray, “Lord, please teach me your way.”

Take a Moment

1. If you were to live as a student, what changes would you need to make in the way that you approach your daily life?
2. What, in your knowledge of God’s truth, do you need to investigate further and understand more fully?

2 | Breathing Violence

For false witnesses have risen against me,
and they breathe out violence.

PSALM 27:12

"Breathing out violence"—perhaps no three words in Scripture more dramatically capture the powerfully damaging presence of sin than these. Imagine a human being, who was made in the image of God, made for loving worship of the Lord and loving community with others, getting to the place where he has fallen so far from God's original intention that he actually exhales violence! You don't have to look very far to see the dramatic damage that sin does to human beings: the high rate of divorce, the violence that is present in every major city in Western culture, the scourge of physical and sexual abuse of children, and something as common as the high level of conflict that exists in all of our relationships in one form or another.

You may be thinking, "Paul, I'm not sure how it's going to help me to think about all of these terrible things." Here's what's important about these three scary words and what they depict: you and I will never understand and celebrate the magnitude of God's transforming grace until we understand the deep damage that sin does to the human heart. You see, sin isn't about human beings being basically okay and just needing a little tweaking in order to be what they were meant to be and do what they were meant to do. No, the damage of sin reaches to every area of our personhood, deeply altering what we think and what we desire.

Isn't it a stunning fact that after Adam and Eve fell, the very next generation was stained with sibling homicide? And consider what Genesis 6:5 says about the impact of sin on human culture. "The LORD saw that the wickedness of man was great in the earth, and that every intention of the thoughts of his heart was only evil continually."

Let that divine report of the damage of sin on the human heart sink in, "that every intention of the thoughts of his heart was only evil all the time!" Could the statement be any stronger?

This is what sin does. Its effect is so pervasive and so comprehensive that it influences everything we do and everything we say. It causes us to think, desire, choose, say, and do things that are the polar opposite of the way we were created to function. So, we don't actually love our neighbor. No, we're jealous of him, or we see him as an obstacle in the way of what we want, or we treat him as an adversary, or we ignore him altogether. And we don't love God with our whole hearts. No, we put creation in his place. We'd rather have the temporary pleasure of physical things than the eternal satisfactions that can be found only in him. Sin causes us to place ourselves at the center of our universe. Sin causes us to be obsessed with what we feel, what we want, and what we think we need.

Sin causes us to set up our own little kingdom of one, where our desire is the functional law of the land. And as little kings, we want to co-opt the people around us into the service of our kingdom purposes, and when they refuse or unwittingly get in the way of what we want, we rage against them. Sometimes it's the quiet rage of bitterness. Sometimes it's the vocal rage of angry and condemning words, and sometimes it's the physical rage of actual acts of violence against another. This is what sin does to all of us.

In light of the fact that sin brings all of us to the point that we exhale violence in some form at some time, it's amazing how much peace and cooperation exist in our relationships. What's the explanation for this apparent contradiction? It can be said in one word: grace. There's not a day where you and yours are not protected by the most powerful, protective, and beneficial force in the universe—the grace of God. Every situation, location, and relationship you're in every day is made livable and tolerable by his grace. In the majesty of his love, God causes his grace to restrain us, just as he causes the sun and the rain to fall on both the just and the unjust. Why does he do this? He does it because of his great love and for the sake of his own glory.

This means that every day you experience the power of his grace. Every day God keeps us all from being as wicked as we have the potential to be. And if he would for a moment withdraw his hand of grace, this world would explode into chaos and violence unlike anything any of us could conceive. You see, you only ever begin to really celebrate grace when you begin to understand how deep and pervasive the effects of sin are. As Jesus said when that woman washed his feet with her hair, "The one who has been forgiven much, loves much."

Take time to consider the ravages of sin on us all, because when you do, you'll leave with a deeper appreciation of grace than you've ever had. And that appreciation won't only cause praise to come out of your mouth, but it will also change the way you live.

Take a Moment

1. How are you dealing with the low-grade or high-intensity anger of those around you?
2. Is there a place where God is calling you to face your own anger, and as you do, what new things is he calling you to do?

3 | Realistic Expectations

> For he will hide me in his shelter
> in the day of trouble.
>
> PSALM 27:5

It's a problem as people face marriage. It's a problem as people think about the workplace. It's a problem as couples anticipate the birth of their first child. It's a problem as we think about our friendships. It's a problem as people think about their life in the church. What is the problem that I'm talking about? It's the problem of unrealistic expectations. Why do we have unrealistic expectations for all of these inescapable dimensions of human life? We have them because we don't take seriously what the Bible has to say about the condition of the world in which we live. Here it is: sin has cast this world into trouble.

There's no escaping it; this world isn't functioning as it was designed to function. The Bible warns us that we're living in a world that's literally groaning, waiting for redemption. We live in a world where disease and death exist, neither one of which was part of the initial plan. We live in a world of deceit and disappointment, neither one a part of God's original intention. We live in a world of rebellion and sin, neither a part of the "good" that God created. We live in a world of suffering and loss, both so far from God's plan. We live in a world of violence and war, surely not the handiwork of the Prince of Peace. We live in a world where lust and greed motivate hearts, not what God intended the heart to do. We live in a world where all of these things touch all of our lives. No relationship is free of disappointment. No institution is totally free of corruption. No location is free of difficulty. No moment in our lives exists untouched by the fall.

Why is this so important to acknowledge? First, much of the

disappointment we face is that we've carried unrealistic expectations into the situations and relationships of our daily lives, and we do that because we have not taken seriously what the Bible says about the fallen world in which we all live. Here's an example I've seen again and again as I've worked with struggling husbands and wives. Couples enter marriage not taking seriously the fact that they're both flawed people, living in a fallen world. Because of this they don't prepare well, as individuals or as a couple, for the difficulties of building a healthy, God-honoring relationship. Consequently, they are caught short and unprepared, as sin within and difficulty without rear their ugly heads in their marriage. Their unrealistic expectations lead to a lack of preparation, which causes them to react rather than act carefully. In the end they are not only suffering the troubles of life in this fallen world, but also they are suffering the fact that they have troubled their own trouble.

All of this creates the tendency for a husband and wife to play to one another's weaknesses instead of their strengths, instead of preparing themselves with the wisdom principles of God's Word and seeking the enabling power of God's grace. God's Word is very, very honest about how broken the world we live in actually is. This honesty is God lovingly helping us to be aware and prepared as we live with one another and wait for the ultimate restoration of everything that is.

But there's something else. Unrealistic expectations cause each of us to live more independently and self-sufficiently than we ever should. In reality, we are all in need of daily rescuing, forgiving, and empowering grace. We need that grace because none of us is free from the presence and power of sin. This means that, moment by moment, we need to be rescued from us!

We also need the grace of God so that we'll be able to love the weak and failing people that we're always in relationships with. But there's something else here. The Word of God is intended to be a "lamp to our feet and a light to our path" (Ps. 119:105). We'll only live properly in this broken world when we're being guided and protected by the light of biblical wisdom in the situations and relationships we live in every day. When I live unaware of how profound my need is and how broken my world is, I don't hunger for the brilliant wisdom of God's Word, and I'm left to my own foolishness. And in my foolishness, I respond to things in a way that only deepens and complicates the troubles that I'm already struggling with.

You can be sure of this; your day of trouble will come. Yet, in your trouble God hasn't left you alone. What is it that he gives you in your trouble? He gives you himself! He is what will keep you safe. He is near, and he comes to you armed with transforming grace and liberating wisdom. But it's vital that you live with eyes and heart open to what Scripture says to you about you and the world in which you live. If you do, you'll live in a way that's humble and needy, seeking the grace and wisdom that you so desperately need and that God so willingly and lovingly gives. Be realistic. Remember, there's amazing grace for every realistic thing you'll be called to face.

Take a Moment

1. Where have you been caught up short because you have failed to live with realistic expectations?
2. What must you do every day to be both realistic and hopeful at the same time?

4 | Fearless Forever

> The LORD is my light and my salvation;
> whom shall I fear?
>
> PSALM 27:1

In a world that is held
in such deep darkness
where the light of truth
often seems more of a flicker
than a flame,
in a world where
deceit
dishonesty
falsehood
and foolishness
divert and distort
the lives of so many,
in times when a myriad
voices
say so
much
about so many things,
where confusion seems
readily available
and clarity seems
hard to find,
in a world where opinions
rise to a place
where only truth should be,
and every voice
seems to get an equal hearing,
in the constant cacophony
of ten thousand
contradictory voices,

it is a wonderful
and amazing thing
to be able to say
with rest and confidence,
The Lord is my Light!
My heart has been lit
by the illuminating
and protective glory
of His
powerful and transforming grace,
my mind has been renewed
by the luminescent presence
of His truth-guiding
Holy Spirit,
and my life has been guided
down straight paths
by the ever-shining lamp
of His Word.
I am not afraid,
but it is not because
I am strong
or wise.
I am not afraid,
but it is not because
I have power
or position.
I am not afraid,
but it is not because
I have health
or wealth.
I am not afraid;
but it is not because
my circumstances
or relationships
are easy.
I am not afraid
for one glorious reason:
I have been lit by the
Lord of Light.
In the darkness
of this fallen world,
I no longer walk

in the night,
but I have been given
the Light of Life.
I am not afraid
because Light lives in me.
This one amazing reality
gives me rest;
I have been rescued from
darkness
and transported into the
light
and I am not afraid.

Take a Moment

1. Where is your living limited or diverted by fear?
2. When you are tempted to give way to fear, what truths about God do you need to remember?

5 | The World's Best Security System

The LORD is my light and my salvation;
whom shall I fear?

PSALM 27:1

It was only the second house we'd ever owned, and we thought we ought to take all the necessary precautions to keep our family, our possessions, and our investment safe. So we contacted the local security company and had them revitalize and update the security system that had been installed in the house by a previous owner. It should be called an insecurity system. Even after the update, it has never quite worked the way it was designed. The crucial motion detector we had installed in the living room malfunctioned quickly. The system is still there, but we never use it anymore.

There are all kinds of security systems that you can look to in your life. Perhaps you look to your investments. You track their growth, and you dream of the life they will provide for you in the future. Yet in your heart of hearts you really do know that there is no such thing as a truly secure investment. Occasionally you do face the fact that you may never experience the comfortable future that you have envisioned because the return on those investments is determined by things that are way outside of your control.

Or maybe your security system is your relationships. You have sought to build around yourself a circle of loving people. You are thankful every day for your family and friends. You find real comfort in their presence in your life and the love they seem to have for you. You do everything you can to make those relationships healthy. Yet in your quiet and reflective moments you know that you can't depend on the permanence of those people in your life. An accident or a disease could remove a loved one very quickly. Sin could do irreparable damage to one of those relationships. A necessary move could put distance between you and someone you thought you'd always have near.

Perhaps your security is in the body of Christ. You are deeply thankful that God has gifted you with a church that has practical biblical preaching and solid Christian fellowship. You should be thankful, but you should also face the fact that on this side of eternity the body of Christ is marred by difficulty. Our family was in a wonderful church that radically changed with the removal of a leader, due to ongoing sin.

Perhaps your security system is actually you. Maybe you live with lots of self-confidence. You had a plan for your life, and so far you have been able to pull it off. You have been able to be successful at the things you have attempted. You have built business and economic success that appears to bode well for your future. You have learned to trust yourself. You have learned to trust your intuition and your instincts, and you have learned when to act fast and when to hold your cards. You are pretty secure with the way that you have conducted your life.

I had an investment banker, who controlled the portfolio of many people, tell me that he was at the top of his game. He had confidence in his own ability, as did many investors. But it all came crashing down with one mistake. His error cost a client his fortune, and his other customers quickly abandoned him.

Or maybe you have no security system at all. Maybe your days are a cycle of concern, fear, and dread. Perhaps you hyper-analyze every decision you make, and you brutalize yourself with doubt after you make them. Perhaps you look with regret at past decisions. Perhaps you give yourself way too much credit for the development of your story. Maybe, if you were able to be honest, you would have to admit that you not only fear people, circumstances, and the future, but you fear something nearer; you fear you. You have no confidence in yourself, and you look at life as a big minefield. You are just working hard to not get blown up!

Deep in our hearts we all know that the typical places we look for security really offer us little of what we seek. That's why this psalm is so practically important. The very first verse of Psalm 27 introduces us to the world's best security system. It isn't to be found horizontally as you scan all the potential places where security can be found. Deep and lasting security, resilient hope, and sturdy rest of heart and mind can only be found vertically. You will only know the rest for which you seek when you begin to embrace the astounding reality of who you are as a child of God. If you are God's child, you are the object of the love of the Person who rules everything that there is to rule.

It's fundamentally impossible to be in a situation, location, or relationship where he is not present. It's impossible for anything to exist outside of the sphere of his control. It's impossible for anything or anyone to be more powerful than him. It's impossible for anything or anyone to be wiser than him. It's impossible for what he desires and has chosen and planned not to come to be. He rules every microbe of physical and spiritual creation. There is no rule of law that stands above him. There is no one to whom he must answer. He is perfect in every way, existing entirely without flaw of will or character. He is the beginning and epicenter of everything that's good, loving, wise, and true. He never forgets, and he never fails to deliver on any of his promises. And Scripture says that he exercises his rule for the sake of his body, the church (see Eph. 2:22–23).

You are secure not because you have control or understanding. You are secure even though you are weak, imperfect, and shortsighted. You are secure for one reason and one reason alone: God exists and he is your Father. He will never leave your side. He will never fail to provide. He will make good on everything he has promised. And he has the power to do so. *He is Lord.*

Take a Moment

1. Where do you tend to look for security? What gives you your inner sense of well-being?
2. What are the things that you need to say to yourself when life seems unpredictable and/or dangerous?

6 | On Christ the Solid Rock

> He will conceal me under the cover of his tent;
> he will lift me high upon a rock.
>
> PSALM 27:5

We all look for it. We all refuse to live without it. We all think we've found it, but it can only really be found in one place. What is it that I'm talking about? Well, here it is: all human beings are on a search somehow someway to find that solid rock on which to stand. That one thing that they can bank on. That one thing that will keep them upright when the storms of life are raging. That one thing that will remain firm for the duration. That one thing that will give them security when nothing else does. That one thing that will give them that deep and abiding inner sense of well-being that every rational human being desires. That one thing that gives them the courage to face what they otherwise wouldn't want to face. That one thing that they can rely on. That one thing that will keep them safe. Everyone is searching for that solid rock.

No human being enjoys feeling that he is living in the sinking sand of unpredictability, disappointment, and danger with no rock to reach for and stand on. In fact, this quest, this desire for surety which is with us every day, points us again and again to the reality of God's existence and our identity as his creatures, his image bearers. We aren't hardwired to live by instinct. Like God, we are in possession of thoughts, desires, and emotions. Like God, we are beings of vision and purpose. Like God, we are spiritual beings. As people made in his likeness, we long for our hearts to be satisfied and our minds to be at rest. We think, analyze, and wonder. We toss our lives over and over again in our hearts, trying our best to make sense of the mystery of our own story and recognizing the scary reality that there's little that we are actually in charge of.

In our honest moments, we know that we couldn't have written ourselves into the situations, locations, and relationships that make up our daily lives. We couldn't have written the story of even one day. Yet we long for our lives to make sense. We long to have meaning and purpose, and we long to have lasting stability.

The problem is that the longer we live, the more we know that there is little around us in this fallen world that's truly stable. I have a wonderful marriage to a lady who in many ways is my hero, but our marriage is still marred by our sin, and this reality still introduces pain and unpredictability into a relationship we have been working on for thirty-seven years! You may think your job is a source of stability, but a bit of a turn in the global economy could have you out on the street in a relatively short period of time. It may seem that your material possessions are permanent, but every physical thing that exists is in a state of decay, and even in its greatest longevity it doesn't have the ability to quiet your heart.

So here is the dilemma of your humanity: you are clearly not in control of the details or destiny of your life, yet as a rational, purposeful, emotional being, you cry for a deep and abiding sense of well-being. In your quest, what you are actually discovering is that you were hardwired to be connected to Another. You weren't hardwired to walk the pathway of life all by yourself. You weren't hardwired to be independently okay. You weren't hardwired to produce in yourself a system of experiences, relationships, and conclusions that would give you rest. You were designed to find your "solid rock" only in a dependent, loving, worshipful relationship with Another. In this way, every human being is on a quest for God; the problem is we don't know that, and in our quest for stability, we attempt to stand on an endless catalog of God-replacements that end up sinking with us.

In fact, our inability to find security for ourselves is so profound that we'd never find on our own the One who is to be our rock; no, he must find us. The language of Psalm 27 is quite precise here: "He will lift me high upon a rock." It doesn't say, "I will find the rock and I will climb up on it."

Here is the hope for every weary traveler whose feet are tired of the slippery instability of mud of a fallen world. Your weariness is a signpost. It's meant to cause you to cry out for help. It's meant to cause you to quit looking for your stability horizontally and begin to cry out for it vertically. It's meant to put an end to your belief that situations, people, locations, possessions, positions, or answers will satisfy the longing of your heart. Your weariness is meant to drive you to God. He is the Rock for which you are longing. He is the one who alone is able to give to you the sense that all is well. And as you abandon your hope in the mirage rocks of this fallen world and begin to hunger for the true Rock, he will reach out and place you on solid ground.

There is a Rock to be found. There is an inner rest to be experienced that's deeper than conceptual understanding, human love, personal success, and the accumulation of possessions. There is a rock that will give you rest even when all of those things have been taken away. That rock is Christ, and you were hardwired to find what you are seeking in him. In his grace, he won't play hide-and-seek with you. In your weakness and weariness, cry out to him. He will find you, and he will be your Rock.

> On Christ the solid rock I stand,
> all other ground is sinking sand.

Take a Moment

1. Be honest as you examine the way you live. What do you look to as your "solid rock"?
2. How would your living be different if Christ really were your "solid rock"?

7 | Sight Problems

. . . that I may dwell in the house of the LORD
all the days of my life,
to gaze upon the beauty of the LORD
and to inquire in his temple.

PSALM 27:4

I've learned so much from George. He has been my friend for over thirty years. He is a man of insight and determination. He has dealt with some of the harshest realities of life in this fallen world. George is blind. The things that George struggles with in his overt blindness have taught me much about the covert blindness of the heart that every sinner struggles with in some way. There is a way in which George's entire life is shaped by recognition of his blindness and by daily strategies to compensate for it. I've learned so much from George.

First, I've learned that there is no more important set of eyes than the eyes of the heart. Yes, George is physically blind, but spiritually he has very good vision. Every day George exercises that mysterious ability that God gives to his children to see the unseen. Now, to people who have embraced the truth that their entire hope in life is centered in a God of grace and glory, who is a spirit, the exercise of this gift of spiritual sight is essential. I've learned from George that your life is always shaped by what your eyes see. If this is true of the physical eyes, how much more is it true of the eyes of the heart?

Second, I've learned how important it is to humbly accept your blindness. George's life is one of courage, hope, and accomplishment precisely because he doesn't live in denial. As a young boy, he confronted the sad reality of his blindness and determined that he would do anything in his power to live, fully live, even though he was blind. Scripture is quite clear about the blinding power of sin. Sin is deceitful, and guess who it deceives first? I have no problem whatsoever seeing the sin of my wife, children, and friends, but I can be quite surprised when mine is pointed out.

Spiritual blindness not only blinds me to the reality of my sin, but it also blinds me to the glory of God that is everywhere around me. God has created his world to be a constant sight-and-sound display of his power, glory, faithfulness, and love. Yet, the eyes of my heart can be so clouded by the duties of the day, by the busyness of the schedule, and by the problems of life that I don't see the God of grace whose glory is evident everywhere I look. Like George, I need to accept that I have a significant sight problem that has the power to radically alter the way I live my life.

Third, I've learned that you always deal with your blindness in community with others. When George got serious about dealing with his handicap, he welcomed people into his life who had the concern, knowledge and skills to help him. Hebrews 3:13 talks about how we need to "exhort one another every day, as long as it is called 'today,' that none of you may be hardened by the deceitfulness of sin." The fact of the matter is this: personal spiritual insight is the product of community. I need people who not only help me see what I couldn't see without them, but who also lovingly help me to admit how blind I actually am and who will teach me how to live—fully live. As long as sin remains in me, I will continue to have pockets of spiritual blindness.

Fourth, I've learned to long for 20/20 vision. George has learned to accept his blindness. He has learned to open himself up to a community of help. He has learned how to compensate for his handicap. But George is not content. He longs for the day when he will be given eyes that see clearly. He looks expectantly for the day when he will no longer be blind.

In the same way, there should be a deep desire in the heart of every sinner to see, really see. We should be tired of being deceived. We should be weary of being blind again and again to the beauty-display of the glory of God that's everywhere around us and that's meant to fill us with a moment-by-moment sense of his presence and grace. We should be tired of the way our lives are bent and twisted by our blindness, tired of the reality that we wouldn't do and say the things that we do if we were really able to see. And we should live for the day when the eyes of our heart will no longer be blind and, with 20/20 vision we will be welcomed to gaze upon the beauty of the Lord forever!

I've learned so much from George. I've learned that I'm more like him than unlike him, and in a profound way, that has changed my life.

Take a Moment

1. Which of the four insights from George's life are particularly needful for you?
2. How could you make greater use of the community of insight that God has placed around you in the body of Christ?

8 | What Is Your One Thing?

One thing have I asked of the LORD,
    that will I seek after:
that I may dwell in the house of the LORD
    all the days of my life,
to gaze upon the beauty of the LORD
    and to inquire in his temple.

PSALM 27:4

It's an incredible statement, one that I'm not sure I could honestly make. It's made even more powerful when you realize that it was written by a man who is under attack. His "one thing" isn't safety, or vindication, or victory. His one thing isn't power, control, or retribution. No, even under personal duress, the one thing that David wishes for is to be in God's house taking in the grandeur and glory of the beauty of the Lord. This desire was designed to be the central motivating desire of every person created by God and made in his image. And yet, on this side of the garden, it seems a statement that could only ever be made by a deeply devout human being.

It does beg the question, "What's your one thing?" What is the one thing that your heart craves? What is the one thing that you think would change your life? What is the one thing that you look to for satisfaction, contentment, or peace? What is the one thing that you mourn having to live without? What is the one thing that fills your daydreams and commands your sleepy meditations? What is your one thing?

The spiritual reality for many of us is that the one thing is not the Lord. And the danger in that reality is this: your one thing will control your heart, and whatever controls your heart will exercise inescapable influence over your words, choices, and actions. Your one thing will become that which shapes and directs your responses to the situations and relationships of your daily life. If the Lord isn't your one thing, the thing that is your one thing will be your functional lord.

Here is what you say to yourself when something is your one thing: "Life has meaning and I have worth only if I have __________ in my life." The problem is that the one-thing catalog[1] is virtually endless:

- *Power.* Life has meaning or I have worth only if I have power and influence over others.
- *Approval.* If I am loved and respected by_______.
- *Comfort.* If I have a certain kind of pleasure or experience.
- *Image.* If I have a certain look or body image.
- *Control.* If I am able to have mastery over a particular area of my life.
- *Dependence.* If someone is there to keep me safe.
- *Independence.* If I am completely free of the obligation or responsibility to take care of someone.
- *Inclusion*: If a particular social or professional group lets me into their inner ring.
- *Achievement.* If I am recognized for my accomplishments.
- *Prosperity.* If I have a certain level of wealth, finance, nice possessions.
- *Work.* If I am highly productive and get a lot done.
- *Religion.* If I am adhering to my religion's codes and accomplished in its activities.
- *Irreligion.* If I am totally independent of organized religion and have a self-made morality.
- *Race or culture.* If my race and culture are ascendant and recognized as superior.
- *A person.* If this one person is happy to be in my life and happy with me.
- *Family.* If my children/parents are happy and happy with me.
- *Helping.* If people are dependent on me and need me.
- *Suffering.* If I am hurting or having a problem, only then do I feel noble, worthy of love, or free of guilt.

You see, in every situation and relationship of your everyday life, there is a one-thing war being fought on the turf of your heart. You and I are safe only when the Lord really is the one thing that commands our hearts and controls our actions. Yet there are many things that compete with him as the one thing that your heart craves.

[1]List adapted from Hannibal Silver (doctor of ministry project, Westminster Theological Seminary)

Where are you looking for meaning and worth? What is the beauty that you wish you had in your life? What is your one thing?

Take a Moment

1. Look at the one-thing catalog. Which of these has tended to hook you? How has that shaped what you do and say?
2. Where do you see a daily war taking place for the control of your heart?

9 | Two Words You Never Want to Hear

Turn not your servant away in anger.
PSALM 27:9

It is such a comfort
to me,
such a source
of hope
and strength
and daily joy.
It gives me reason
to get up in the morning
and to press on
even
when I am discouraged
and weak
and lonely
and afraid.
It gives me reason
to face with courage
the struggles within
and the difficulties without.
It reminds me
that I can stand
before You
as I am,
completely unafraid
and ask of You
what I have asked before
and will ask again:
Your forgiveness
and Your help.

What gives me this
courage?
What offers me this
hope?
It is this one thing.
I know for certain
that there are
two words
that I'll never hear.
I know that You will never
look me in the eye
and say to me,
"Go away!"
You will not send me
from Your presence.
You will not drive me
from Your grace.
You will not separate me
from Your glory.
You will not eliminate me
from Your promises.
You will never
ever
ever
send me away.
Because Your anger
was borne by Another.
Because my separation
was carried by Him.
Because He was
sent away,
I will never be.
So, in weakness,
failure,
foolishness,
and sin,
I stand before You once more
with courage,
hope,
comfort,
and joy,
because I know

that in all the
dark things that
may be whispered to me
in this dark and fallen world
there are two words I will never hear.
And so with gratitude and joy
I get up to face the day
but as I do, I do it
without fear.

Take a Moment

1. Do you live with the fear that you will do or say something that would cause God to say to you, "Go away"?
2. Name some ways that the fear of God's anger and rejection shapes the way that you respond to him, to others, and to circumstances.

10 | Sign Beauty

> . . . To gaze upon the beauty of the LORD
> and to inquire in his temple.
>
> PSALM 27:4

God has filled His world with beauty.
There is the beauty of:
the delicate orchid
the spotted leopard
the multi-hued sunset
the pillowy cloud
the golden sun
the delicious meal
the giant oak
the iridescent snake
the white-capped wave
the ribbony grain of wood
the song of a bird
the endless variety of music
the flash of lightning
the shimmering scales of a fish
the new white snow
the rugged rocks of the mountain
the tender kiss
the whisper of the breeze
the green curtain of the leaves
the security of a father's voice
the tender touch of a mother's hand
the crystal display of a starry night
the percussive song of a rainy day
the green of the pasture
the blue of the sky
the black of the night
the brown of the soil

the yellow of the bee
the red of the rose
the white of the cloud.

All of those things have been painted with beauty, but it is not ultimate beauty. The beauty of the created world was never meant to be the beauty that would fill the eyes of our hearts. It was never meant to be the beauty to which we would look for satisfaction and peace. It was never meant to be the beauty that we would give ourselves to search for, live for, cry for, and die for. No, the physical glories of this created world are meant to be sign glories. The amazing beauty that surrounds us every day was designed to be sign beauty. All of the beautiful things that we see, touch, taste, and hear every day were designed to be signs that would point to the ultimate beauty that can be found only in the One who created them.

So when you are looking at the beauty that surrounds you in the physical world that is your present home, require yourself to look beyond the signs to the stunning beauty of the God to whom each sign points. Only his beauty can give you hope, strength, and peace. Only his beauty can give you life. Don't be like the family that saved for a year to experience the glories of Disney World, packed the car in anticipation, drove hundreds of miles, and stopped at the first Disney World sign and had their vacation.

When we look to our husband or our wife for our identity, we are stopping at the Disney World sign. When we look to our job for our meaning and purpose, we are stopping at the Disney World sign. When the acceptance and respect of friends is what gets us up in the morning, we are stopping at the Disney World sign. When we look to material possessions to give our hearts peace and rest, we are stopping at the Disney World sign. When we look to theological knowledge and ministry skill to satisfy our hearts, we are stopping at the Disney World sign. When we look to our children to fulfill us, we are stopping at the Disney World sign. When in moments of pain, we turn to food, alcohol, TV, or the Web, we are stopping at the Disney World sign. When a day in nature means more to us than a half-hour in personal worship and prayer, we are stopping at the Disney World sign.

Perhaps our hearts feel empty and our souls are dissatisfied because we have tried to get from sign beauty what only ultimate beauty can give us. Look beyond the orchid, the lightning, the bird, and the leaf and see the Lord. In him you will find true beauty, the kind that really does satisfy.

Take a Moment

1. For further study, go to John 6 and the miracle of the feeding of the crowd of five thousand. What was the purpose of the miracle? What happened after? What mistake were the people making?
2. What "sign" do you have a tendency to look to for your identity, meaning, and purpose rather than the Lord, to whom that thing points?

11 | Inner Strength

> Wait for the LORD;
> be strong, and let your heart take courage;
> wait for the LORD!
>
> PSALM 27:14

On this side of eternity you and I are called to wait. We are called to recognize that the most important, most essential, most beautiful, and most lasting things in our life are things over which we have no control. No, these things are the gracious gifts of a loving Father. He never is foolish in the way he dispenses his gifts. He never plays favorites. He never mocks our neediness. He never plays bait and switch. He never teases or toys with us. His timing is always right, and the gifts that he gives are always appropriate to the moment. He is kind, faithful, loving, merciful, and good.

The One on whom we wait is a dissatisfied Messiah. He will not relent, he will not quit, he will not rest until every promise he has made has been fully delivered. He will not turn from his work until every one of his children has been totally transformed. He will continue to fight until the last enemy is under his feet. He will reign until his kingdom has fully come. As long as sin exists, he will shower us with forgiving, empowering, and delivering grace. He will defend us against attack and will attack the enemy on our behalf.

He will be faithful to convict, rebuke, encourage, and comfort. He will continue to open the warehouse of his wisdom and unfold for us the glorious mysteries of his truth. He will stand with us through the darkness and the light. He will guide us on a path we could never have discovered or would never have been wise enough to choose. He will supply for us every good thing that we need to be what he has called us to be, and to do what he has called us to do in the place where he has put us. And he will not rest from his work until every last microbe of sin has been completely eradicated from every heart of each of his children!

Yet, with all of this being true, we find it hard to wait. We aren't always "strong" in our waiting. No, waiting for many of us becomes a time for increasing fear, doubt, discouragement, and susceptibility to temptation. As faith grows weak, our resolve begins to dim, and we begin to secretly wonder if it's worth it to obey.

Why? Why do we struggle to be "strong and let [our hearts] take courage" when we are being called to wait? Perhaps the answer is found in Romans 4:18–21 (NIV):

> Against all hope, Abraham in hope believed and so became the father of many nations, just as it had been said to him, "So shall your offspring be." Without weakening in his faith, he faced the fact that his body was as good as dead—since he was about a hundred years old—and that Sarah's womb was also dead. Yet he did not waver through unbelief regarding the promise of God, but was strengthened in his faith and gave glory to God, being fully persuaded that God had power to do what he had promised.

Why did Abraham grow stronger in faith as he waited those many long years? It isn't because he played mental denial games. No, the passage makes it very clear that he faced the facts of the situation head on. In his time of waiting, Abraham had a very different experience than we often do, because Abraham did something that we often fail to do. Here it is: the temptation, in times of waiting, is to focus on the thing we are waiting for, all the obstacles that are in the way, our inability to make it happen, and all of the other people who haven't seemed to have had to wait. Along with this we rehearse to ourselves how essential the thing is and how much we are daily losing in its absence. All of this increases our feeling of helplessness, our tendency to think our situation is hopeless, and our judgment that waiting is futile.

While it's true that Abraham considered the facts, they weren't the focus of his meditation. No, his focus was on the God who had made this promise. Every day Abraham would get up and remind himself that the God who had made the promises on which he was waiting was absolutely able to deliver them. The God who made heaven and earth would have no trouble causing an old woman to deliver a promised child! Abraham didn't fill his mind with his own weakness and the seeming futility of the situation. No, he filled his mind again and again with the glory of God's immeasurable power, and as he did, he grew stronger and stronger in faith.

Somewhere in your life you are being called to wait. In your waiting, you are being given an opportunity to deepen and strengthen your faith. So, get up tomorrow and fill yourself with vitamins of truth. Nourish your heart with the nutrient food of the glory of God. Feed on the strength-giving meat of his goodness, grace, and love. Snack throughout the day on his power and his presence. And watch the muscles of your heart grow stronger as the days go by. Feed on your Lord and be strong!

Take a Moment

1. Where, right now, are you finding it hard to wait?
2. What would it look like for you to "snack throughout the day" in order for the difficulty of waiting to become an occasion of strength?

12 | Goodness

> I believe that I shall look upon the goodness of the Lord in the land of the living!
>
> PSALM 27:13

I have one place of confidence,
one place of rest
and peace
and hope.
I have one place of surety,
where courage
can be found
and strength
waits for the taking.
I have one place of wisdom
where foolishness wanes
and truth grants freedom.
Alone I am not confident,
no pride in strength
or knowledge
or character.
I know who I am,
the duplicity of my heart,
the weakness of resolve,
the covert disloyalty
that makes me susceptible
to temptation's hook.
I have one place of confidence;
it isn't a theology
a book
a set of principles
a well-researched observation
a worldview.
No, my confidence is in You.

You are my hope because
You are Good.
I rest in the goodness of Your
sovereignty,
in the goodness of Your
power,
in the goodness of Your
faithfulness,
in the goodness of Your
wisdom,
in the goodness of Your
patience,
in the goodness of Your
mercy,
in the goodness of Your
holiness,
in the goodness of Your
grace.
I have learned
and I am learning
that the physical delights
of the created world
were not designed to be
the source
and hope
of my confidence.
No, all of those things
in their temporary elegance
were meant to be
signposts
that point me to the
eternal
never-failing
always available
never-changing
always holy
grace-infused
goodness that can only be found
in You.
I have learned
and I am learning
that confident living

always rests its foundation
on You.
I am confident
because of this solitary thing,
You are
and You are good.

Take a Moment

1. List ten ways that the goodness of the Lord is evident in your life.
2. Where have you been tempted to question God's goodness?

13 | Why Would God Ever Answer Me?

Hear, O Lord, when I cry aloud;
be gracious to me and answer me!
PSALM 27:7

I never get used to the moment-by-moment miracle of prayer. It's an amazing thing that God would ever even once listen to me, let alone answer! In little moments and big, again and again, I choose my own kingdom over his. I often run to him for help for messes that in my foolishness and rebellion I've made. I've no righteousness to present as an argument that he should hear me. I've no autonomous wisdom that I can present as a reason for his attention. I've no independent track record of good deeds that would get his attention.

I've often been more fickle than loyal. I often justify my sin rather than seek his forgiveness. I struggle more with being attracted to the temporary pleasures of this physical world than I am committed to godly living. The desires of my heart wander again and again. I forget my identity as his child, and in my amnesia I seek identity where it was never meant to be found. Again and again I contradict the theology that I say I believe with the way that I live. I sadly have to ask for his forgiveness for the same things over and over again. Undeserving is the way I always stand before him.

This is precisely why David appeals to God's mercy as he prays. He can't look to himself for any reason that God would listen and respond. Yet, the miracle of his existence and ours is that he doesn't have to fear God's rejection or fall into thinking that prayer is an exercise in spiritual futility. Why? Because God is his own reason for answering. Prayer finds its hope not in the qualifications of the one praying, but in the character and plan of the God who is hearing.

He answers because of who he is. He answers because of what he is doing. He answers because he loves to see us come, and he loves to provide just the grace for that moment.

Maybe you are thinking, "Paul, be more specific. Why exactly would God respond to me?" Here are five reasons:

1) *His love.* He's the ultimate wise, patient, kind, gentle, and forgiving father. He delights in his children. Because of his great love, his eyes look out for us and his ears are always attentive to our cries. Because of his love, he invites us to bring our cares to him, and he assures us that he really does care for us. He is never too busy or distracted or too tired to hear and answer. He doesn't refuse to answer because of our weakness and failure. He doesn't get impatient because we have to come again and again. He is love, and he loves to exercise his power and glory to meet the needs of his struggling children.

2) *His grace.* Grace provides the whole structure and standing of our relationship with him. If it weren't for the grandeur of his forgiving grace, we would have no relationship with him at all. Because of his grace, he is unwilling to rest until the work of transformation is complete. In grace he looks on us and knows that this work isn't done. We've not yet been completely formed into the likeness of his Son. Although the power of sin has been broken, he knows that the presence of sin still remains. He hears our prayers because, when we pray, we confess that we still need the grace of forgiveness and deliverance, and in so doing we place ourselves in the center of what he has committed himself to complete—his work of redemption.

3) *His faithfulness.* He doesn't change his mind. He doesn't ride the roller-coaster of the rise and fall of emotions. His heart isn't a battle zone of conflicting motivations. He doesn't get bored, exhausted, or distracted. He won't quit what he has begun. He won't forsake those upon whom he has placed his love. He won't harden his heart, shut down his mind, and turn his back. He won't take a break or go to sleep. He will never tell you that you have asked too much or that you have come to him too often. You never have to work to figure him out. You never have to wonder if his response to you will change. He is absolutely faithful to every promise he has made and every provision he has offered. Your hope in prayer is rooted in his faithfulness, not yours.

4) *His kingdom.* As I come to him in the patterns laid out by Christ and pray, "Your kingdom come, your will be done on earth as it is in heaven," I pray words that bring him delight. He loves the exercise of his will. He finds joy in the success of his kingdom. The spiritual growth and prosperity of his children means the growth and prosperity of his kingdom. He is King, and he delights in his children's recognizing his lordship and submitting to his rule. Every good thing he does for his children is done to rescue them from their self-focused kingdom of one and to welcome them into the expansiveness of his kingdom of glory and grace. And his ears will continue to be attentive and his hands will be active until his kingdom has been fully and completely established forever.

5) *His glory.* The thing that God is most committed to is his own glory. But here's what you need to understand. His commitment to his own glory is your only hope. Because he is committed to his own glory, he has committed to draw to himself a multitude of people who forsake their own glory and do the one thing that they were created to do: live for his. So his commitment to his glory causes him to listen and respond, listen and respond until all of his children no longer look to the shadow glories of creation for their satisfaction but, rather, look to him. Because he is committed to his glory, I can go to him in prayer, knowing that he will hear and answer.

So even though you have nothing to bring to the Lord that would commend you to him, you can approach him with confidence. He really does delight in hearing and answering his children. Your hope in prayer is never found in you; it is always found in him.

Take a Moment

1. How healthy is your life of prayer? What keeps you from praying as you should? What changes need to take place?

2. Look at the five reasons for being confident in prayer. Are there doubts about them in your heart?

14 | You're Talking to Yourself

> My heart says to you,
> "Your face, LORD, do I seek."
>
> PSALM 27:8

I find myself saying it all the time. When people hear it they laugh, but actually I'm being quite serious when I say it. Here it is: no one is more influential in your life than you are, because no one talks to you more than you do. You are in an unending conversation with yourself. You are talking to yourself all the time, interpreting, organizing, and analyzing what's going on inside you and around you.

You may be talking to yourself about why you feel so tired. Or maybe you woke up this morning with a sense of dread and you are not sure why. Perhaps you were surprised by how angry you got at the remark of that coworker. Or maybe you are rehearsing to yourself your schedule for the day, wondering why you agree to so many things in one day. Perhaps you are reliving a conversation that didn't go too well. Or maybe you are preparing yourself for a conversation that may be difficult, conjuring up as many renditions as you can imagine so you can cover all the contingencies. Maybe your mind has traveled back to your distant past and, for reasons you don't understand, you are recalling events from your early childhood. Or maybe you are simply telling yourself to buck up, slow down, hang in there, or take charge.

The point is that you are constantly involved in an internal conversation that greatly influences the things you decide, say, and do. In Psalm 27, David lets us eavesdrop on his internal conversation. He is exhorting himself, in the midst of his trouble, not to run away from God but to run toward him. Now that's good self-counsel!

What do you regularly tell yourself about yourself, God, and your circumstances? Do your words to yourself encourage faith, hope, and courage? Or do they stimulate doubt, discouragement, and fear? Do you remind yourself that God is near, or do you reason within yourself, given your circumstances, that he must be distant? Do you encourage yourself to run to God even when you don't understand what he is doing? Or do you give yourself permission to back away from him when you are confused by the seeming distance between what he has promised and what you are experiencing? Are you your own best defense lawyer, laying out arguments for your innocence in places where you are actually guilty? When others talk to you, is your internal conversation so loud that it's hard to concentrate on what they are saying?

Here's the question: how wholesome, faith-driven, and Christ-centered is the conversation that you have with yourself every day? Do you remind yourself of your need? Do you point yourself, once again, to the beauty and practicality of God's grace? Do you tell yourself to run toward him in those moments when you feel like running from him? Would you be comfortable with someone's playing a public recording of the private conversation you have with yourself every day?

No one is more influential in your life than you are, because no one talks to you more than you do. How well are you counseling yourself? Reach out for help one more time today. Confess that you don't counsel yourself very well, and rest in the rescuing grace of the One who is called Wonderful Counselor.

Take a Moment

1. What are the things that you regularly say to yourself that shape the decisions you make, the actions you take, and the words you say?
2. What are some of the truths from Psalm 27 that you can call to mind as you talk to yourself?

15 | The Shortest Distance between Two Points

> Teach me your way, O LORD,
> and lead me on a level path
> because of my enemies.
>
> PSALM 27:11

My dad was the guru of shortcuts. He lived on an endless quest for the shortest route to all of the places to which he regularly drove. My mom used to kid my dad that most of his shortcuts were in fact "longcuts." In his search for the shortest distance to wherever, my dad would say again and again, "The shortest distance between two points is a straight line."

The life to which God has called us is the ultimate straight line. This line starts with dead rebels and ends with people alive and reformed into the likeness of God's Son. The problem is that our living is seldom a straight line. We all take daily detours of thought and desire that move us off the straight path that God has placed us on by his grace. He has redeemed us from the jungle of our rebellion, lust, autonomy, foolishness, and self-focus and placed us on the narrow pathway of his Son. The problem is that we all tend to get tricked into taking detours that get us off God's path and into trouble.

Our problem is twofold. First we get diverted because we are impatient. The trip to where God is taking us is not an event; it's a process. And the process isn't easy. God's road takes us through the heat of the sun, through storms and cold, through the dark of night, through loneliness and confusion. So, we get tired and impatient and begin to convince ourselves that there is a better way. But, that isn't all.

We get diverted because we are disloyal. Our hearts aren't yet fully committed to God's glory and his kingdom. We are still attracted to the shadow glories of creation, and we still carry around in us allegiance to the small-agenda purposes of the kingdom of self. So in our impatience and disloyalty we see pathways that appear easier and more comfortable, but they only ever lead to danger.

There is no time when this temptation is more powerful than when we are facing difficulty. This is exactly what the verse we are considering recognizes. When you are being hammered by the enemy, it's very tempting to debate within yourself as to whether God's way is the best way. It starts with bad attitudes. Perhaps you begin to doubt God, doubt his goodness, and question his love. Perhaps you give way to anger, impatience, and irritation. Or maybe you begin to allow yourself to envy. You wonder why the guy next to you has such an easy life, when yours is so hard.

These bad attitudes lead to bad habits. You quit praying because you reason that it doesn't seem to be doing any good. You stop reading your Bible because those promises don't seem to be coming true in your life. You quit attending your small group because you can't stand to hear the stories of God's love that others share, when your life is so hard. You even begin to give yourself reasons for missing the Sunday worship service, reasons you once wouldn't have given yourself. Before too long there is a coldness and distance in your relationship with God that would have shocked you in the early days of your faith. Your difficulty has deceived you into thinking that you have reason for wandering off God's straight path, and your attitudes and habits have placed you on the dangerous side-paths of the kingdom of self.

Have you gotten off God's straight path? Have you given yourself reason to take side-paths? How about praying, once again today, "Teach me your way, O Lord, and lead me on a level path"?

Take a Moment

1. Where have impatience and disloyalty gotten you off God's path?
2. As you have been waiting, what new things has God taught you about yourself, himself, life in this fallen world, sin, and his grace?

16 | Mercy Prayer

Hear, O LORD, when I cry aloud;
be gracious to me and answer me!
PSALM 27:7

I have no resumé
to hold before You,
no track record of accomplishments,
no letters of commendation,
no rights of birth or ethnicity.
I hold nothing
that would place You in my debt,
nothing
that could curry Your favor,
nothing
that would obligate You.
I wish unbridled zeal
would commend me to You.
I wish unbroken obedience
would draw Your attention.
I wish model wisdom and model love
would convince You that I'm worthy.
But I have none of these things
to offer You.
I stand before You with shoulders bent
and hands that are empty.
I approach You with no
argument in my mind
or words to offer in my defense.
I stand before You
naked and undeserving,
broken and weak.
I am quite aware of the
duplicity of my heart,
the evil of my choices,
and the failure of my behavior,
but I am not afraid

because I stand before You
with one argument,
with one plea.
This argument is enough.
This plea is sufficient.
This argument is the only thing
that could ever give me
courage,
rest,
and sturdy hope.
So I come before You
with this plea:
Your mercy.
Your mercy is my rest.
Your mercy is my hope.
Your mercy makes me bold.
Your mercy is all I need.
Your mercy
tells me You will hear.
Your mercy
tells me You will act.
Your mercy
tells me You will forgive.
Your mercy
tells me You will restore.
Your mercy
tells me You will strengthen.
Your mercy is my
welcome,
plea,
and rescue.
I rest in this one thing:
You are mercy
and
You will answer.

Take a Moment

1. Are you resting in God's mercy or still working to perform your way into his acceptance?

2. Where in your life do self-reliance and self-righteousness keep you from humbly seeking the mercy of the Lord?

17 | Uber Music

I will sing and make melody to the LORD.

PSALM 27:6

While the minor-key music
of the fallen world
drones on
sung by the choir
of the lost,
the blind,
the deceived,
the wounded,
the poor,
the weak,
the rebel,
the lame,
the willful,
and the enslaved,
singing the sad notes
of a world
once beautiful,
now broken,
of hearts
once pure,
now corrupted,
of darkness
where light was meant to be,
of death,
where life was meant to flourish,
of slavery
where freedom was designed to reign,
You have given me
a song to sing.
It is a song
of boundless love.

It is a song
of rescuing grace.
It is a song
of tender mercy.
Its verses tell
how redeeming hands
touched a broken world,
giving life again
giving freedom again
giving peace again
giving hope again
giving broken hearts
a reason to sing again.
Its chorus swells
to heights never before sung
and its constant refrain
is
Alleluia,
Alleluia to the Lamb,
Alleluia.
Your grace
has placed in my mouth
the only song worth singing.
Your love
has placed on my tongue
the only words worth repeating.
Your mercy
has returned to my heart
the only music worth playing.
It is the song of songs,
and one million years
into eternity
it will be
as beautiful and new
as the moment
the first note was sung.

Take a Moment

1. What circumstances of life have silenced your song of celebration and worship?

2. Write your own song of grace; what lines of praise will you pen?

18 | Take Heart

> Be strong, and let your heart take courage;
> wait for the LORD!
>
> PSALM 27:14

You've heard it said many times, "Take heart: this too will pass," or "Take heart: it's not as bad as you think it is," or "Take heart: you love one another; this will eventually work out." Usually when you hear the words "take heart" someone is trying to make you feel better about something that has gotten you down. Maybe it's a tough circumstance that you are having to endure, a hurtful moment in a relationship, or a disappointment you have to face.

The "take heart" response of the person who is near you is an attempt to temporarily alter your feelings about the thing that has upset you. The person speaking means well, but the "take heart" they offer you doesn't really offer you much to hold on to. You stand in the middle of something that's bigger than you and over which you have no control, and you are invited to hope that it isn't as bad as it seems. Well, that's an offer of hope that, when examined, doesn't really give you any concrete reason to be hopeful.

Psalm 27 ends with a "take heart," but this "take heart" offers a very different hope than what we often offer one another in moments of difficulty and disappointment. What makes this "take heart" different is that it's a call to wait on the Lord. It isn't about trying to change emotions; rather it's an invitation to rest in the one place where rest can really be found—in the Lord.

Who is this One in whom you can take heart?

First, he is the definition of love. Scripture says something amazing about the love of God. It doesn't simply say that God is committed to faithful love. It doesn't just say that God loves you even when you don't deserve his love. It doesn't only say that he loves you better than anyone else will ever love you. No, what the Bible says about God can't be said about anyone else. It says that "God is love." God is the essence, the source, the ultimate definition of love, and love that is true love has God as its source. If there was no God, there would be no love. I can take heart because my life is held in the hands of the One who is the essence of love.

Second, he is the source of all wisdom. In Colossians 2, the apostle Paul says that "all the treasures of wisdom and knowledge are hidden in Christ." Think how radical this is. As believers in Jesus Christ, we know that wisdom isn't an outline, a theology, or a book. We know that wisdom is a Person and his name is Jesus. You get true wisdom not by experience, education, or research, but by relationship. When you come to Christ you are now in a personal relationship with the One who is wisdom. You can take heart because the One who holds you defines everything that wisdom is about.

Third, he is a God of awesome power. How do you do justice to describing the power of God? There is nothing to which it can be compared. There are no analogies to it to be found anywhere in the created world. The thunderstorm, the tempestuous sea, the hurricane, and the tornado with all of their great power contain an infinitesimal fraction of the power of God. This is the One who created the world and everything that's in it. This is the One who holds the world together simply by the exercise of his will. When you rest in him, you can take heart because he really does have the power to deliver everything he has promised you.

Fourth, this is a God of unchallenged rule. In Daniel 4 we are reminded that God rules over the "host of heaven and the inhabitants of earth." We are further reminded that no one has the authority to stop his hand or question what he does. God is in absolute control over the world he made. What he wills happens. His plan will be done. His kingdom will be established. He won't lose any of the children he has chosen to be his own. When I'm in difficulty and I run to God, I'm running to the One who is in absolute control of every circumstance that appears to me to be out of control. Now that's a reason for taking heart!

Fifth, he's a God of glorious grace. God's grace means that I can rest assured that I'll have everything I need to be what he wants me to be and to do what he wants me to do in the situation in which he has placed me. I'm no longer restricted to the limits of my own strength and wisdom. By his grace, I have a new identity and a new potential. I'm a child of God; the risen Christ now lives inside me. I need no longer fear people or circumstances; I don't have to feel weak in the face of suffering or temptation, because I no longer rest in the resources of my own ability. I'm in Christ and he is in me. This new identity gives me new potential as I face the realities of life in this bent and broken world. God's grace gives me reason to take heart.

When I'm in difficulty and I take heart in the Lord, rather than be weakened by the difficulty, I grow stronger. The more I meditate on the glory of God, the more my faith grows; the more my faith grows, the more I respond to life with hope and courage; the more I respond to life with hope and courage, the more I harvest the new fruit in concrete changes in the situations and relationships that I am facing.

If you are God's child, you have reason to take heart, no matter what you are facing.

Take a Moment

1. What situations and relationships are you facing right now that are tempting you to lose heart?
2. As you consider the listed reasons to take heart, which are you most tempted to forget?

19 | Not Yours

> My heart says to you,
> "Your face, LORD, do I seek."
>
> PSALM 27:8

I cannot say my heart is pure,
no,
not because it is riddled with lust
or
stained with hatred,
but because
it does not always long for You.
My heart longs
for comfort and ease,
for power and control,
for possessions and position,
for acceptance and recognition.
It longs for so many of the things
that carry the promise of
satisfaction
contentment
happiness
joy.
Yet, my heart is wired for You,
wired
to rest only in the rest found
in You.
It would be easy to reason
that I am okay.
I am not a thief.
I am not a murderer.
I have not stolen the spouse of another.
But this reality I cannot escape:
my heart is not pure,

because it does not always
long for You.
I have hated in my heart.
I have stolen with my thoughts.
I have lusted in secret.
I have done all these things
because my heart
doesn't always belong to You.
Lord, once more draw my heart to You.
Capture my thoughts.
Command my desires.
Submit my will.
Direct my plans.
Make my heart pure,
not because it is free of struggle,
but because
it no longer seeks
identity
meaning
peace
purpose,
that inner sense of well-being
in You.
When my heart finds life in You,
it will no longer
seek it in another.
I wish I could say I am pure,
but the battle still rages,
and rescue is still needed,
so that the longings of my heart
will not pull me away,
but will draw me
ever closer
to You.

Take a Moment

1. What does your heart long for other than the Lord? How does that longing shape the way you live?
2. If longing for the Lord ruled your heart without challenge, how would your living be different?

20 | Sinned Against Again

Though an army encamp against me . . .

PSALM 27:3

Your Lord has chosen to keep you here in this world, so bent and twisted by the fall. He has chosen you to live in an environment where there is no perfection to be found. He has chosen you to live as a flawed person among flawed people. He has chosen to keep you where injustice, corruption, jealousy, greed, anger, and conflict are everyday occurrences. He has not coated you with situational Teflon, protecting you from the disappointments and hurts of a world gone bad. There is no way you and I will avoid being sinned against. There is no way we will escape being besieged. God's covenant promises to you don't include a "being sinned against" exemption clause.

So, what do you do when you are sinned against—again? Wives, what do you do when your husband comes home and treats you harshly? Husbands, what do you do when your wife seems more demanding than thankful? Parents, how do you respond when your children make a mess of the great family day you'd planned? Workers, how do you deal with the fact that that fellow-worker has been speaking negatively about you to your boss? What do you do when no one notices how well you have served? What fills your thoughts when that friend has proven to be disloyal once again? How do you deal with family injustice and favoritism? What do you do when the irresponsible choices of others have altered your life, maybe even for the long run? You see, you will not escape these experiences. Your life won't be free of interpersonal trials, and you will respond to them daily in some way.

What is the typical way you respond to being sinned against? Do you give way to fear, trying to conceive of all the possible "what ifs," as if figuring out what could happen will protect you from it actually happening? Do you tend to wallow in the "if only's" of what could have been, wishing for outcomes that have already passed you by? Do you bunker down and determine to live self-protectively, telling yourself that you have been taken once and it won't happen again? Are you tempted to strike back in anger, wanting others to hurt in the way that they have hurt you? Do you tend to slip into your cocoon of silence, refusing to deal with the person who has hurt you? Do you speak and act in haste? Do you allow the failure of others to initiate a new round of doubtful thoughts about the Lord, his love, mercy, and grace?

What do all of these reactions have in common? They make what happens to you the most important thing in your life. They make your disappointment the saddest thing in your life. They make your feelings the most accurate indicator of how good your life really is. Yet, here's the truth of what's happening in those moments of being sinned against: you have been called to endure those experiences because of the choices of another.

You and I are not in control of our lives; we are not the writers of our own stories. Our individual stories have been embedded in the story of another. We are not the chief actor in the drama that is our own lives. The decisions of someone else are driving the plot of each of our stories. No, I'm not talking about the person who has mistreated you; I'm talking about your Lord. You're facing what you are facing not simply because of the sin of that other person, but because of the wise choice of a loving Redeemer.

The fact is that God has us exactly where he wants us. He never manages a poor schedule, and he never gets a wrong address. He places us in interpersonal difficulty because he intends that difficulty to be a workroom of redemption. This was exactly what Joseph understood when he endured the life-altering injustices of his brothers. Hear his words: "As for you, you meant evil against me, but God meant it for good, to bring it about that many people should be kept alive, as they are today" (Gen. 50:20). Because this is true you can respond to being sinned against in brand-new ways.

Let me suggest four God-centered, grace-recognizing ways to respond to being sinned against.

1) *Run to the temple*. Run to your Lord, not away from him. Instead of meditating on all the nasty things that you have endured at the hands of the person who hurt you, give yourself to examining, meditating upon, and recounting the beauty of your Lord. Let your

mind consider his love, mercy, grace, patience, faithfulness, gentleness, wisdom, power, forgiveness, and kindness. Require yourself to consider that this moment may not be a contradiction of his character qualities, but rather a demonstration of them.

2) *Remember your place.* Your life no longer belongs to you. Your story is no longer just your story. You have been welcomed to the kingdom of another, and your life is part of the plan and purposes of that kingdom. Don't allow yourself to begin to think that you are in the center of your universe. Remember, you have been chosen to live for the glory of another, and when you do, you will reach levels of personal contentment and joy that aren't possible any other way.

3) *Learn your lessons.* God has you in the painful moment not simply to reveal himself to you but to grow and change you through it, as well. He has chosen to keep you in this fallen world because he hasn't finished redeeming you. Sure, you long for the grace of release and the grace of relief, and sometimes you do experience these, but primarily this moment is a moment of refinement. The heat of interpersonal difficulty is meant to purify us, something that each of us continues to need.

4) *Reflect his light.* In these painful experiences, God is not only calling you to submit to his will but to actively give yourself to the values and work of his kingdom. He calls you to reflect the light of his character. He calls you to suffer in ways that can only be explained by his presence and power in your life. Jesus said it this way: ". . . that they may see your good works and give glory to your Father who is in heaven" (Matt. 5:16).

Remember, you are not alone, and what is happening to you isn't an accident. You are the child of the King of kings, the Creator, the sovereign God, the all-wise and all-loving Savior. In ways that are hard to grasp, you are being loved. Rest in that love and run to its source, saying no to all those other responses that only add further trouble to the trouble you are already experiencing.

Take a Moment

1. What are the things you typically do when you are sinned against?
2. Of the four things suggested, which are you most tempted to forget when your life is troubled by the sin of others?

21 | The Pursuit-of-God Paradigm

> Teach me your way, O LORD,
> and lead me on a level path
> because of my enemies.
>
> PSALM 27:11

Your life is more organized than you think. No, I don't mean that you make good use of your smartphone or your PDA. And I don't mean that you are able to successfully control your schedule so that your days are orderly and predictable. What I mean is that your life is organized around the pursuit of something. You are not as spontaneous and reactive as you might think. Your sudden impulses may not be as impulsive as you think they are. Your snap decisions are probably more thought through than you realize. You are living for something, and that something is a powerful organizing force in your life.

Confused? Well, journey with me back to the beginnings of human life in the garden. You can know significant things about the nature of human beings and how they function if you pay attention to what happened in humanity's early moments. Immediately upon creating Adam and Eve, God began to talk to them. Why? Because, unlike the rest of animate creation, people do not live by instinct. People's lives are directed by the thoughts and motives of the heart. Every person is a theologian. Every person is a scientific researcher. Every person is a philosopher. Every person is an investigator. Every person is developing a functional view of life that becomes the tool by which he or she makes sense out of what is and what is experienced.

People are also beings of purpose. They are moved by passions and desires. They live in pursuit of treasures to which they have assigned value. There are things they crave and things they detest. They run after things they love and run from things they hate. They find joy in the acquisition of what is a treasure to them and experience disappointment when their treasures slip through their fingers like sand.

This is why God immediately talks to Adam and Eve. He knows the kind of creatures he has made, so he immediately begins to define for them the paradigm that is to shape their living. He tells them what to think and what to desire. Those early words make it very clear that Adam and Eve were created by God and were designed to live for God. This means that everything they were to do as human beings was to be shaped by their love for, worship of, and obedience to God. That is what the Bible calls "God's way." It is the unique lifestyle that will shape the actions, reactions, and responses to life of a person who acknowledges God's existence, character, and plan.

But there is another way of living that structures people's lives as well. It is what Proverbs calls "a way that seems right to a man" (14:12; 16:25). Eugene Peterson makes the observation that there is a replacement trinity for the true Trinity. It is holy wants, holy needs, and holy feelings. When I live by this trinity my life is functionally organized by what I want (some earthly thing that has become my treasure), what I tell myself I need (this treasure rises in influence until I am convinced I cannot live without it), and holy feelings (an emotional life that is dictated by how close I am to possessing the treasure that I have set my heart on). Here, too, I am never really spontaneously reacting to life. What seem to be impulsive reactions are shaped by wants, needs, and feelings that attach themselves to the treasure I crave.

It is important to recognize that there is a war being waged in my heart between these two paradigms. Sometimes I get it right, and my life really is structured by a pursuit of God, a rest in his grace, and obedience to his plan. But other times I am driven by my selfish cravings, convincing myself that I cannot live without this thing that I am so zealously pursuing. It is also important to recognize that God's paradigm brings life, and man's paradigm leads to death. It is only when my life is shaped by a pursuit of God that I can live with a heart that is satisfied and at rest.

Your life really is more organized than you think. What paradigm shapes your responses to life and structures your day? Don't be afraid to confess that you often get it wrong. Your Lord not only offers you his forgiveness, but he also fights for your freedom. So you can say, "Lord, so often I get it wrong; won't you teach me your way once more today?"

Take a Moment

1. What "treasures" tend to claim your heart and set the agenda for your life?
2. Where have your wants, needs, and feelings set more of the agenda for you than the call of the Lord in his Word?

22 | Safe

> For he will hide me in his shelter
> in the day of trouble.
> PSALM 27:5

I am safe,
not because I have no
trouble,
or because I never experience
danger.
I am safe,
not because people affirm
me,
or my plans always
work out.
I am safe,
not because I am immune from
disease,
or free of the potential for
poverty.
I am safe,
not because I am protected from
disappointment,
or separated from this
fallen world.
I am safe,
not because I am
wise
or strong.
I am safe,
not because I deserve
comfort or have earned my
ease.
I am safe,

not because of
money
or power,
or position,
or intellect,
or who I know,
or where I live.
I am safe because of the glorious mystery of
grace.
I am safe because of the presence of
boundless love.
I am safe because of
divine mercy,
divine wisdom,
divine power,
and divine grace.
I am safe,
not because I never face
danger,
but because You are
with me in it.
You have not given me
a ticket out of danger.
You have not promised me
a life of ease.
You have chosen to place me in
a fallen world.
I am safe
because You have given me
the one thing
that is the
only thing
that will ever keep me safe.
You have given me
You.
I am safe
from my evil heart
and this shattered world,
not because I can escape
them both,
but because in the middle of
temptation and trial,

danger and disappointment,
sickness and want,
You give me everything
I need to
fight temptation
and avoid defeat
and to point others
to the safety
that can be found only
in You.
So, I will wake up tomorrow
and face the anxiety
of not knowing
the fear of my own weakness,
and the reality of the fall.
I will live with
faith,
courage,
perseverance,
and hope.
And when danger comes,
and it will,
I will whisper to
my weakening heart,
"Emmanuel is your shelter;
you are safe."

Take a Moment

1. Where in your life is God exposing the inadequacy and unreliability of the places to which you have looked for safety?
2. Humbly consider if there is a person or thing that you would rather have in your life than the security the Lord has promised you in his care.

23 | The Delusion of Independence

> Hide not your face from me.
> Turn not your servant away in anger,
> O you who have been my help.
> Cast me not off; forsake me not,
> O God of my salvation!
>
> PSALM 27:9

Do you view yourself as a person in need of help? Do you seek to live more independently than you should? How do you respond when God sends someone your way to correct or confront you? Do you bolster yourself with evidences of your righteousness, or do you regularly look in the mirror of the Word of God and admit how needy you actually are? Do you live with a sense of need for the heart-educating classroom of grace or do you think of yourself as a grace graduate? Do you think of others as needier than you? Even as you minister to others, do you think of yourself as one in need of ministry as well? When you seek to understand why you do the things you do, do you look outside or inside yourself for the answer?

One of the sad results of sin is that it causes all of us at some time and in some way to buy into the delusion of independence. Independence is what the serpent sold Adam and Eve, but this independence was as counterfeit as the proverbial three-dollar bill. The counterfeit currency of independence is the reward that the enemy continues to wave in front of each one of us. The lie goes this way: "You can be whatever you want to be and do whatever you want to do." This lie is designed to make me believe that I'm wiser and more righteous than I actually am. It makes me think that I'm a mature person living in a colony of the immature. It causes me to reason that if I do bad things, I do them not because of what's inside of me, but because of the pressures that I am forced to deal with that are outside of me. This lie is meant to convince me that I'm capable and okay.

Here's what the Bible makes blatantly clear; the quest for independence never ends in independence. It always ends in slavery. Why? Because I was carefully designed by the Creator to live in a dependent, obedient, and worshipful relationship with him and in humble, interdependent relationships with other human beings. The quest for independence is not simply a spiritual mistake; it's a fundamental denial of my humanity. The pursuit of independence always leaves me addicted to a list of things that I've looked to for hope, life, strength, and rest. In a vain attempt to distract myself from the evidence that I'm not, in fact, independent, I get hooked on things that have the ability to distract me but can never give my heart rest.

The message of Psalm 27 and the rest of the Bible is clear: I'm a person in desperate need of help, and if I walk with God for thousands of years I will continue to need his help as much as I did the first day I reached out my hand for him.

Does the way you relate to members of your family picture a person who believes that he is in daily need of help? Does the level of your commitment to Christian fellowship depict a person who thinks she is in need of help? Does your personal devotional life paint a portrait of a person who humbly acknowledges his need of help? Is your life a picture of the celebration that will result when you begin to grasp that, by the grace of Jesus Christ, you have been brought into personal relationship with the only source of the kind of help that you truly need—God himself? Do you love God's truth, love his people, love his gatherings of worship, love the work of his kingdom, and love the hymns of his grace, all because you have humbly acknowledged the depth of your need and joyfully embrace the heart-transforming reality of his help?

The only way you will ever run to the Helper is by running away from the delusion of independence. Why not do that once more today?

Take a Moment

1. In what ways are you living as if you are more independent than you actually are?
2. Where have you tended to blame "inside" sins on the situations and relationships that exist outside of you?

24 | Singleness of Focus

One thing have I asked of the LORD,
that will I seek after:
that I may dwell in the house of the LORD
all the days of my life,
to gaze upon the beauty of the LORD
and to inquire in his temple.

PSALM 27:4

Do you live with singleness of focus? Is your life shaped, structured, and directed by the pursuit of one glorious, fulfilling, heart-satisfying thing? Or is your life a picture of a constantly changing narrative of fickle affections careening from one hope to the next?

You see, you don't live by instinct. Your life is directed by the thoughts and motives of your heart. You are always interpreting, and you are always desiring. You live in perpetual pursuit of something. You are always evaluating your progress toward that thing that you think will give you life. You are always in the possession of and in the service of some kind of dream. Maybe this is the best way to say it: you are living for something.

Scriptures like Psalm 27 and Matthew 6:19–33 remind us that all the things for which a human being could live fall into two categories. The first category is the *Creator* category. When I am living for something in the Creator category, I'm living for what can be found only in God. It means my life is shaped and directed by my resting in the pursuit of his grace, glory, goodness, and plan on earth. Another name for this category is the *kingdom of God*.

The second category is the *creation* category. When I am living in the creation category, I'm seeking to find my identity, meaning, and purpose in something that has been created. So, I look to my job, friends, possessions, or a position to satisfy my heart. Another name for this is the *kingdom of self*.

What does all of this have to do with singleness or fickleness of focus? It is only when I'm hooking my life to the glory and grace of God and getting my identity from him that I can truly live with singleness of focus for the long run. This is because it is only God who has the power to satisfy my heart. I was made for him. I was made to have my life shaped by an acknowledgment of his presence, a rest in his love, and an active allegiance to his purposes. When I live this way, my soul is satisfied and my heart is at rest.

On the other hand, when I seek to satisfy my heart by the pursuit of a seemingly endless catalog of God-replacements, my heart will be anything but satisfied. So, I will abandon one dissatisfying creation dream for another, only to have that one leave me empty as well. I'll run from my friends to my job or possessions in the frantic pursuit of what can be found only in the Lord. My life will be characterized by fickleness rather than singleness of focus because it was created to be satisfied in God alone.

Is your life shaped by one great desire, a desire for the Lord? Or is it a picture of the constantly changing focus that is the result of asking the creation to offer what only the Creator can give? Your heart will rest only when he is the one thing that gives your life focus.

Take a Moment

1. What pursuit forms your reason for deciding, doing, and saying the things you do?
2. How would your responses to daily situations and relationships be different if you were hooking them to the glory and grace of God?

25 | The Worship of Another

I will offer in his tent
  sacrifices with shouts of joy;
I will sing and make melody to the LORD.
PSALM 27:6

Sacrifices,
I don't want to have to make
sacrifices.
I want my plate
full
and my schedule
empty.
I want to be with people
I like,
people who are low in
maintenance and high in
appreciation.
I want control over
my time
my energy
my money
my things.
I want my days to be
predictable
and my plans
unobstructed.
I want to experience
success
and successfully to avoid
failure.
I would rather be served than
to serve.
I would rather get the gift than

to give.
I guess this all points me to
one stunning reality.
There is never a day when
my life is
idol-free.
There is never a week
when I don't give myself to the worship
of another.
It is sad to say
and humbling to admit,
that the chief of these
false deities
is none other than
me.
I am the sovereign
I want to serve.
I am the king
I want others to obey.
I am the lord
I want to rule my days.
Yes, it is true,
Dear Father,
I want to be
You.
My dissatisfaction is not because
You are not
wise
faithful
loving
good,
but because I do not get
my own way.
So, once more I
bow,
once more I make my
confession,
once more I plead for
mercy
pardon
power
deliverance.

Once more I ask,
Dear Savior,
Please free me
from me
and cause this selfish heart
to find
joy
satisfaction
motivation
delight
in doing the
one thing
I was given breath
to do:
offer myself as a
sacrifice
in the service of
You.

Take a Moment

1. Where, right now, is God calling you to personal sacrifice of time, energy, and/or money for the sake of his kingdom?
2. What thing in your life are you holding to too tightly? Where do you wish you were sovereign so that you could guarantee that something you want remains in your life?

26 | The Rejection of Rejection

My father and my mother have forsaken me,
but the LORD will take me in.
PSALM 27:10

Unthinkable
irrational
impossible to conceive.
The Trinity
torn asunder.
The Son
wrenched from His Father.
Salvation realized.
I am
the liar.
I am
the thief.
I am
the gossip.
I am
the rebel.
I have wanted
my own way
in
my own time
at
my appointed place.
I have rebelled
against Your law
and I have
set up my own.
I deny
Your kingship
while building

a kingdom of my own.
I think
my wisdom
is wiser than You.
I think
my plan
is better than Yours.
I crave
the sovereignty
that only You should have.
But You did
the inconceivable;
You accomplished
the undoable.
You stood
in my place
and You satisfied
God's wrath.
But
in the process,
the Three in One
was torn in two.
In the process,
the Father
did the most painful thing
that has ever been done.
He turned His back
on You.
You withstood
this pain
so that I would never have to.
You took my
rejection
so that I would only ever have
acceptance.
So, I can
rest assured,
I can
live in hope,
I can
enjoy true peace,
because I know

that You are always with me.
For long ago
on the cross
Your rejection
was for me
the final rejection of rejection.

Take a Moment

1. In what ways would your practical, daily living change if you lived with a deep and lively sense of appreciation for the horror of the rejection Jesus faced for you?
2. Where is God calling you to offer to others the same love and grace that you have been given?

27 | Spiritual Muscles

> Wait for the LORD;
> be strong, and let your heart take courage;
> wait for the LORD!
>
> PSALM 27:14

When God asks you to wait, what happens to your spiritual muscles? While you wait, do your spiritual muscles grow bigger and stronger or do they grow flaccid and atrophied? Waiting for the Lord isn't about God forgetting you, forsaking you, or being unfaithful to his promises. It's actually God giving you time to consider his glory and to grow stronger in faith. Remember, waiting isn't just about what you are hoping for at the end of the wait, but also about what you will become as you wait.

Waiting always presents me with a spiritual choice-point. Will I allow myself to question God's goodness and progressively grow weaker in faith, or will I embrace the opportunity of faith that God is giving me and build my spiritual muscles?

It's so easy to question your belief system when you are not sure what God is doing. It's so easy to give way to doubt when you are being called to wait. It's so easy to forsake good habits and to take up habits of *unfaith* that weaken the muscles of the heart. Let me suggest some habits of unfaith that cause waiting to be a time of increasing weakness rather than of building strength.

Giving way to doubt. There's a fine line between the struggle to wait and giving way to doubt. When you are called to wait, you are being called to do something that wasn't part of your plan and is therefore something that you struggle to see as good. Because you are convinced that what you want is right and good, it doesn't seem loving that you are being asked to wait. You can see how tempting it is then to begin to consider questions of God's wisdom, goodness, and love.

Giving way to anger. It's very easy to look around and begin to think that the bad guys are being blessed and the good guys are getting hammered (see Psalm 73). There will be times when it simply doesn't seem right that you have to wait for something that seems so obviously good to you. It will feel that you are being wronged, and when it does, it seems right to be angry. Because of this, it's important to understand that the anger you feel in these moments is more than anger with the people or circumstances that are the visible cause for your waiting. No, your anger is actually anger with the One who is in control of those people and those circumstances. You are actually giving way to thinking that you have been wronged by him.

Giving way to discouragement. This is where I begin to let my heart run away with the "If only_____," the "What if_____," and the "What will happen if_____." I begin to give my mind to thinking about what will happen if my request isn't answered soon, or what in the world will happen if it's not answered at all. This kind of meditation makes me feel that my life is out of control. Rather than my heart being filled with joy, my heart gets flooded with worry and dread. Free mental time is spent considering my dark future, with all the resulting discouragement that will always follow.

Giving way to envy. When I am waiting, it's very tempting to look over the fence and wish for the life of someone who doesn't appear to have been called to wait. It's very easy to take on an "I wish I were that guy" way of living. You can't give way to envy without questioning God's wisdom and his love. Here is the logic: if God really loves you as much as he loves that other guy, you would have what the other guy has. Envy is about feeling forgotten and forsaken, coupled with a craving to have what your neighbor enjoys.

Giving way to inactivity. The result of giving way to all of these things is inactivity. If God isn't as good and wise as I once thought he was, if he withholds good things from his children, and if he plays favorites, then why would I continue to pursue him? Maybe all those habits of faith aren't helping me after all; maybe I've been kidding myself.

Sadly, this is the course that many people take as they wait. Rather than growing in faith, their motivation for spiritual exercise is destroyed by doubt, anger, discouragement, and envy, and the muscles of faith that were once robust and strong are now atrophied and weak.

The reality of waiting is that it's an expression of God's goodness. He is wise and loving. His timing is always right, and his focus isn't so much on what you will experience and enjoy, but on what you will become. He is committed to using every tool at his disposal to rescue you from yourself and to shape you into the likeness of his Son. The fact is that waiting is one of his primary shaping tools.

So, how do you build your spiritual muscles during the wait? Well, you must commit yourself to resisting those habits of unfaith and with discipline pursue a rigorous routine of spiritual exercise. What is the equipment in God's gym of faith? Here are the things that he has designed for you to build the muscles of your heart and strengthen your resolve: the regular study of his Word; consistent godly fellowship; looking for God's glory in creation every day; putting yourself under excellent preaching and teaching of Scripture; investing your quiet mental time in meditating on the goodness of God (e.g., as you are going off to sleep); reading excellent Christian books; and spending ample time in prayer. All of these things will result in spiritual strength and vitality.

Is God asking you to wait? What is happening to your muscles?

Take a Moment

1. Where, right now, is the God of grace calling you to wait?
2. Which habits of *unfaith* are most tempting for you? What is God calling you to do to resist these temptations by his grace?

28 | The Back of God's Head

> Hide not your face from me.
> Turn not your servant away in anger,
> O you who have been my help.
> Cast me not off; forsake me not,
> O God of my salvation!
>
> PSALM 27:9

It is a wonderful thing for every child of God to know that the one thing he will never, ever see is the back of God's head. God will never hide his face from us. He will never turn his back on us. He will never turn and walk away. He will never reject or forsake us. He will never cast us off. Perhaps the most glorious mystery of our lives is that we have been chosen to have his face forever toward us. We have been chosen to have his smile forever on us. We have been blessed to have him look on us with love and grace forever and ever!

What is stunning about the favor of God is that we could never have done anything to deserve, achieve, or earn it. I was irritated with my wife yesterday; no, not because she is a sinner and not because she did anything wrong. No, I was irritated because she didn't fit as well within my sovereign plan for the day as I wanted. In an instant I began to look at the one human being that I love most on this earth as an obstacle rather than as an object of my affection.

It wasn't long before I was filled with remorse and a sense of how deep my need still is for the rescuing grace of the Lord. You see, what stunned me about the favor of the Lord isn't just that there was a period in my life long ago when I got it all wrong and when I wanted to be my own king. No, even as God's child I still get it wrong. I still have moments when I'm much more excited about my kingdom than

I am about God's. I still forget the glorious reality of his love for me and hook my life to the flawed glories of the created world.

Yet, in all of this God doesn't get exasperated. He doesn't grow weary. He doesn't wonder why in the world he redeemed me in the first place. He doesn't look for ways to show me how much I have hurt him. He doesn't harbor bitterness or hold a grudge. He doesn't hide his face or run or walk away. He is patient in love and persevering in grace even though I still am not able to earn his favor.

Why am I so blessed? I am blessed because, in the most painful moment in human history, Jesus willingly subjected himself to the rejection of his Father. He took on my sin and allowed himself to be rejected. In this unthinkable moment of substitution, the Trinity was torn apart as the Father turned away from the Son. Here is what you and I have to understand: Jesus was willing to suffer the horrible rejection of his Father so that you and I would never, ever have to experience it ourselves.

Jesus willingly looked at the back of God's head so that we would never look at anything but his face. So, today, when you envision God with the eyes of your heart, envision his face, because if you are his child it is the only thing you are ever going to see.

Take a Moment

1. Do you fear God's rejection? How does this fear tend to shape the way you live?
2. How would the way you approach life change if you lived with a picture of God's face of love in your heart day after day?

29 | Under Attack

When evildoers assail me
    to eat up my flesh,
my adversaries and foes,
    it is they who stumble and fall.
PSALM 27:2

Under attack again.
Such is life
in a broken world
where sin still
lives
where the enemy still
lurks
where broken
things
and broken
people
do not do the things
they were made to do.
Under attack again.
Why was I surprised?
Why did I give way
to anger
to fear
to discouragement
to vengeance
to questioning
the one thing that is
sure
safe
constant
reliable?
You have promised

to keep me
to protect me
to nurture me
to love me
to defend me
to defeat my foes.
I have rested
in the hollow of Your hand.
I have hidden
under the shelter of Your wing.
I have had Your peace
put me to sleep.
I have had Your presence
comfort my heart.
I have had Your Spirit
give me new strength.
Yet somehow
when under attack again
I forgot You
and in forgetting
I did what I
regret.
I said what gives me
grief
I even questioned
You.
The enemies I face
are too great.
The brokenness around me
is too pervasive.
The sin inside of me
I cannot escape.
So I have come home again,
home to this one thing
I daily need
in moments
mundane and great,
the rescue that
can be found only
in You.
I know that in the face of
Your wisdom

Your control
Your power
Your righteousness
the enemies of my soul
will stumble
will fall
will crumble in defeat.
When evil comes
and it will,
I will
remember You
run to You
believe in You
rest in You
and with
hands that are clean
and a
heart that is pure
I will fight evil,
not with words
of evil
or actions
of vengeance
but with the one thing
the enemy cannot defeat—
worship of You.

Take a Moment

1. Is there a place in your life where you are under attack? How are you responding?
2. What evidence is there in your life that sometimes you tend to forget the safety of the protecting grace of your Savior?

30 | Someday

> I believe that I shall look upon the goodness of the LORD in the land of the living!
>
> PSALM 27:13

"Someday, maybe, someday." We have all said it, but it's not really a statement of hope. It's more often a fatalistic resignation to the death of some kind of dream.

"Someday I'll get a decent job."

"Someday we'll be able to afford the kind of house our family really needs."

"Someday I'll get myself in shape."

"Someday I'll finally find a good church."

"Someday I'll find that special person to love."

"Someday we'll get our finances in order."

"Someday I'll go back to school."

"Someday I'll quit saying 'someday.'"

"Someday" is a way of communicating what we wish would happen, but deep down inside we don't really think it will. We say it because it makes us momentarily feel better about the things in the here and now that we have trouble accepting.

The reason our somedays are more fatalistic than hopeful is that in our sane moments we all know that we don't have the power and control over our world that we would need to have in order to guarantee the realization of our dreams. We also know that we are harvesting the choices we have made that have led us to where we are. So our somedays are more medicinal and therapeutic than hopeful predictions of what surely will come. They are mental pills to get dissatisfied hearts through disappointing days.

The someday of Psalm 27 is very different. It is a statement of confidence that is both deeply encouraging and powerfully motivating. When David says that someday he will see "the goodness of the LORD in the land of the living," he isn't caressing some future dream in order to help himself accept present disappointment. In fact, this statement isn't a wish or a dream at all. It's not really a hope for some future outcome. No, what David makes here is a statement of *identity*. David is remembering who he is, and in remembering who he is, he is remembering what he has now and in the future.

Who is David? He is a child of the God of Israel. He is one of God's chosen, the object of God's love, the recipient of God's promises. The God who is his Father is a God of immeasurable power, unfathomable wisdom, inconceivable sovereignty, untainted truth, and abounding grace. David's God isn't only the ultimate definition of what is good; he also has the power and control to produce every good thing that he has promised his children.

He is in absolute control of every location, circumstance, individual, natural force, institution, and relationship. As Nebuchadnezzar said, after being humbled by this God, "he does according to his will among the host of heaven and among the inhabitants of the earth; and none can stay his hand or say to him, 'What have you done?'" (Dan. 4:35).

Trust in God isn't a thin hope in some not very sure outcome. Hope in God is rather a present investment in a future guarantee. What God says will be done. What God has promised will come to pass. His word is reliable because in his grace he wants to bless us, and in his power he has the ability to do anything he has promised to do. When you live with his promises in view, you live with confidence, courage, and unshakable hope.

You then become free of anxiety and worry. You become free of vain attempts to manipulate people and situations in order to get what you want. You place yourself in the hands of a sovereign God of grace who knows exactly what you need, when you need it, how you need it, and where you will need it. And because your Father is good, he will never turn a deaf ear to your cries, and he will never abandon you in your hour of need. No, you won't always understand what he is doing, and you will be tempted to think that he has gotten his timing wrong, but the more you entrust your life to him, the more you will experience his faithful grace again and again.

Who holds your someday? Are you still attempting to change things that are beyond your power and out of your control? Have you simply given up and in your disappointment are you resigned to play mental dream games to keep yourself going? Look up! Your Father controls it all, and he looks on you with grace and favor. It is never ever risky to place your past, present, and future in his hands. His someday isn't a *someday* at all; no, it's a *will be*.

Take a Moment

1. Where do you tend to forget your identity as a child of God?
2. Where in your life do anxiety and worry reveal that, in the press of life in this broken world, you tend to forget the "goodness of God," which you are guaranteed as his child?

31 | The Theology of Beauty

. . . That I may dwell in the house of the LORD
all the days of my life,
to gaze upon the beauty of the LORD.
PSALM 27:4

Beauty.
What is beauty?
How is beauty?
Where is beauty?
Is beauty without a
beginning?
Is beauty without an
end?
Could it be that there are
only
two kinds of beauty?
In this world there is
Source beauty
and
Reflected beauty.
Source beauty is
true beauty
pure beauty
timeless beauty
independent beauty
definitional beauty
divine beauty.
Reflected beauty is
shadow beauty
tainted beauty
dependent beauty
ill-defined beauty
creation beauty.

All sin is sin against
beauty.
Idolatry puts
Reflected beauty
in
Source beauty's place.
Sin hammers Reflected
beauty
into the shape of
ugly.
Sin then names ugly
beautiful.
The more distant it is from its
source
the less beauty there is to be
found
in Reflected beauty.
Source beauty is not to be
manipulated
or
ignored.
It is only
ever
eternally to be
worshiped.
In the
Incarnation
the feet of beauty
touched earth
to reveal
beauty
to teach
beauty
to restore
beauty
to help beauty be
seen
experienced
worshiped
loved
in order that
in the hearts of men

Source beauty
would be restored
to its
rightful place.
But
I still live
in the middle of
a beauty war.
And in the fog
of the
conflict
I do not see beauty
clearly.
With battle scarred
eyes
I look at what is
ugly
and I think I see
beauty.
Please heal
my eyes.
Please restore
my heart
so I may
gaze nowhere else
but
see
love
worship
the beauty
that only
ever
emanates
from You.

Take a Moment

1. Is there a place in your life where you are tempted to look at what God says is ugly and to see beauty?
2. When do you tend to get so captivated by the "reflected beauty" of the created world that you are blind to the "source beauty" of the glory of the God who made it?

32 | One Beauty

> One thing have I asked of the LORD . . .
> that I may dwell in the house of the LORD . . .
> to gaze upon the beauty of the LORD.
> PSALM 27:4

One thing,
One thing,
One thing!
It's hard to imagine
One thing
When I seem to be attracted
to so many things.
It is a continuing
struggle.
It is a daily
battle.
It is my constant
war.
The world of the physical
attracts me
excites me
magnetizes me
addicts me.
I confuse consumption
with satisfaction.
I confuse satisfied senses
with true joy.
I confuse a stomach that is full
with a heart at rest.
Sometimes I would rather have
my appetites satisfied
than a grace-filled heart.
Sometimes I would rather hold

the physical
than have the eyes of my heart
be filled
with the beauty of
the spiritual.
I am tired of seeing
only what
my physical eyes
can see.
I want eyes
to see
what
cannot be seen.
I am tired of craving
people
possessions
locations
circumstances
positions
experiences
appearances . . .
Somewhere in my heart
I know that only You
satisfy.
Deep in my heart
I want You to be
enough.
I must quit
moving
running
driving
pursuing
consuming.
I need to
stop.
I need to
be quiet.
I need to sit
in the seat of grace
and wait
and wait
until these blind eyes

see
until this cold heart
craves
the one beauty that
satisfies
the one beauty that
is You.

Take a Moment

1. What things in this physical, created world tend to attract, distract, and capture you and, because of that, set the agenda for how you live?
2. Where do you tend to confuse the satisfaction of consumption with a heart that is spiritually filled?

33 | Wanting What Is Right When You Are Wronged

When evildoers assail me . . . one thing . . .
PSALM 27:2, 4

If an army of evil men were out to assail you, if there was a plot against you to end your life, what would you want, what would you do? The response of the psalmist here is significant and challenging. When you are being wronged, when a family member, a neighbor, a member of the body of Christ, or a coworker has wronged you or is in some way out to get you, it is so easy to lose your way. It is so easy to drop the good things that you have been doing, things that protect your heart and nurture your soul. It is so easy to meditate on evil and forget what is good, true, beautiful, and wholesome.

Perhaps for you, losing your way means allowing your mind to be consumed with playing over and over again a mental DVD of what someone said or did. Perhaps it means allowing yourself to give way to the fears of what in the world could happen next. Maybe losing your way means fantasizing about how you could settle the score, you know, the things that you would like to say and do to that person that would make him hurt the way he has hurt you. Maybe losing your way means that you allow your hurt and dismay to take you away from good habits of personal devotion and ministry. Or sadly, perhaps losing your way means beginning to doubt God, his promises, his presence, and his love.

I wish I could say that in the face of mistreatment, I had never lost my way, but I can't. I was a young pastor. I was doing everything that I could to grow and exercise the teaching gift that God had given me. But there was a critical man in our congregation who seemed never to be satisfied. One evening he came to me and said, "Paul, your preaching is killing us!"

Now, these are happy words for a young pastor to hear. I said, "Well, what do you suggest?"

He handed me a set of tapes and said, "I suggest listening to these."

Naïvely I said, "And what do you think I should get out of the tapes?"

He said, "Just mimic the preacher on the tapes and that will be better than what we have been getting."

I don't think I realized how hurt I was. I know I did think I had lost my way. But the very next Sunday, when I got up to speak and looked out at the congregation, everyone's head was the normal size, except for my critical friend. To me his head looked to be the size of a fully inflated beach ball. I seemed unable to ignore his reactions. It seemed impossible to avoid his critical gaze. I think I hated that man, and I know I was determined to do anything I could to convince him that I was a good preacher. But in so doing, I was no longer preaching to honor God and his calling. I was no longer preaching for the spiritual benefit of the congregation. I was no longer working to prepare content that was true to the text; I was preparing content that I thought would finally silence my enemy in the fifth pew.

But my preaching got worse. I was fearful and nervous. I stumbled over my words. I was not confident with my content. I was a mess, and I was increasingly discouraged. I didn't know it, but in my hurt and distress I had run from the Lord rather than to him. I thought winning would heal my heart, but my heart would only be healed, confident, and satisfied when it was filled with the love of the Lord. The acceptance of this man would never be achieved, and if it were, it would not satisfy my heart.

At the end of the morning service one Sunday, I noticed the oldest lady in our congregation hanging around, waiting to talk. I waited until the crowd had cleared and asked her what she wanted. She said, "Paul, I don't want to talk about me; I want to talk about you. Over the last few weeks I have become concerned about your preaching. You have lost all of your confidence. I have become convinced that someone has gotten to you and that you are preaching to please that person and not the Lord." I couldn't believe what I was hearing!

Then she said, "Monday, you get up, forget that person, and

study God's Word, and then you preach what God has given you with confidence and joy or we're all in trouble." And she turned and walked out of the church.

At that moment I knew she was right. In the face of mistreatment, I had lost my way. I had not run to the Lord. I had not allowed my heart to be healed by his grace and my confidence to be restored by his presence. I had decided I would beat my "enemy" at his game. I had decided that I would win. And it left me with an empty heart and a mouth that was unable.

I did get up the next morning and confess my sin. And I did enter that next Sunday with excitement at the truths that God had given me to share. And it was not long before my critical friend left the church.

I would ask you one question: "When you are wrong, where do you run?" There is only one place where your heart can be healed, restored, satisfied, and protected. It won't be healed by winning human wars. It won't be satisfied in human acceptance. It won't be restored when you have meted out vengeance. It will only be filled, satisfied, and at rest when it is filled with the beauty of the Lord.

Take a Moment

1. In what way do you tend to lose your way when you are being wronged?
2. If your heart was satisfied by Christ, how would your response to being wronged change?

34 | People in Need of Help

> Hide not your face from me.
> Turn not your servant away in anger,
> O you who have been my help.
> Cast me not off; forsake me not,
> O God of my salvation!
>
> PSALM 27:9

Do you ever feel overwhelmed? Do you ever feel that the tasks that God has given you are too big for you to do? Do you ever feel that God has gotten a wrong address? How do you go about assessing your need of help?

It's something all human beings do—it's called "measuring your potential." We all do it often. The little toddler who is standing on newly mobile legs looking across the room at his daddy as he holds onto his mother's knee, is measuring his potential to make it the five steps from Mommy's knee to Daddy's knee. The teenager who's driving to his first day at his first job, holding the steering wheel with clammy, nervous hands, is measuring his potential to do well enough in this new world of employment without getting himself quickly fired. The bride who has an upset stomach as she is having her hair coiffed is measuring her potential to live in lifelong intimacy with another human being.

A person normally measures his potential based on two factors. The first is his track record. He does a quick scan of his life, assessing how he has done so far. He looks to the past to give him some kind of read on his potential for being successful in the present. He next examines the size of the task. Does he have what it takes to take on a task of this size?

While there is some logic to this way of assessing personal potential, the little phrase in verse 9, "O you who have been my help," reveals to a believer the inadequacy of this kind of assessment. The problem is that it doesn't account for your new identity, and therefore, your new potential as a child of God.

God is the ultimate helper. He alone has the grace to rescue you from yourself. What does this mean? He gives you power to deal with all the sins of thought and desire that get in the way of your doing what God has called you to do.

Not only does he help you with internal weaknesses, but he alone is able to remove external obstacles. Because he is our helper, we don't have to place the completion or success of the task on our shoulders. It's not our job to complete the task; it's our job to obey God's call. He will complete the task. I don't have the power to get people to respond. I don't have the power to make situations change. I can't make my spouse love me. I can't get my children to believe. I can't force two people to reconcile. I can't make my neighbor be committed to peace. It's not my job to make these things happen. It's my job to respond to the call of God in each of these areas; the hearts of people and the control of situations are in his hands.

His promise is that when we go, he goes with us. He will never call us to do a task without giving us what we need to do it. He is unshakably committed to meeting the needs of his people. He is unshakably committed to the success of his kingdom. Since you are his child, wherever you go, his presence and power go as well. He really is with you always, and he really is the helper that you need.

So how are you measuring your potential? Are there places where you are living more in fear and avoidance than with courage and hope? Are there places where you feel completely overwhelmed? Could it be that as you have assessed your potential you have forgotten who your helper is? You are now personally connected to the ultimate source of help. How's that for potential?

Take a Moment

1. In the busyness of your daily situations and relationships, where do you tend to forget how deep and consistent your need actually is for God's daily help?
2. List the ways that God has promised to be your helper.

35 | Watch Out for the Flesh Eaters!

When evildoers assail me
    to eat up my flesh,
my adversaries and foes,
    it is they who stumble and fall.

PSALM 27:2

I wish that it were
peacetime
but
right now
you can't live that way.
Temptation is all around.
It's a smile
a whisper
a wish
an invitation
a sword.
There's little escape,
so little time to rest,
evil flirts with you
but will consume your flesh.
Do you really think
you're not at risk?
Has your enemy
lost his power
to tempt
to seduce
to ensnare
to trap?
Do you really have
the liberty

to coast
to rest
to relax, to slide on through?
When no day is an escape
there's seldom rest,
evil hungers for you
to digest your flesh.
There is war being made;
darkness and light
truth and lie
right and wrong
wise and foolish
holy and sin
God and the Devil
demon and Friend,
So there's little escape
there's precious little rest,
evil lurks out there
it will eat your flesh.
This world
is shattered glass.
It does not look
It does not do
as designed.
You are infected
with the disease.
You are flawed
from within.
Sin still lives.
It is a law
a war
a prison
a trap
a drug.
Not many roads of escape
really not much rest
evil sings to you
but will devour your flesh.
There is but one
escape.
Just one thing
you can do.

Focus your eyes on
what you see.
Fix your gaze.
Look at the beauty
the treasure
the majesty
the glory
the Lord.
Run to the temple
Be in awe.
Be enthralled.
Meditate.
And remember
what's holy
what's eternal
what's gorgeous
what's true.
Bask in the beauty
It will rescue you.
Because there's little escape
there's a famine of rest,
evil waits for you
but will dine on your flesh.
May beauty be
your fortress.
May glory be
your rock.
May the Lord be
your refuge
Until the war
is over
Until you've arrived
at rest
Until evil has been
crushed
and you're home at last.
For there's scant escape
there's a real lack of rest,
evil hunts for you
to consume your flesh.

Take a Moment

1. Do you tend to forget that, this side of eternity, there is a great spiritual war being fought inside and outside of you? Do you forget it in your marriage or in your parenting? Do you forget it in friendship, in work, in material things?

2. What evidence in your life indicates that you are living with a peacetime mentality rather than with preparedness for spiritual conflict?

36 | Why I Hate to Wait

Wait for the LORD;
be strong, and let your heart take courage;
wait for the LORD!

PSALM 27:14

I hate to wait;
I have places to go
I have people to see
I have things to do.
I love me
and I have a wonderful plan
for my life.
I hate to wait.
I don't like obstacles
in my way
or people that disagree
or processes that take too long.
I hate to wait.
I don't like lines
or traffic
or delayed appointments
or tardy people.
I hate to wait.
I wake up every day
with an agenda.
I know
what I want to accomplish.
I know
how I want it done.
I know
where I want it done.
I know
when I want it done.

I know
who I want to do it.
I know
why it has to be done this way.
I hate to wait
because
I am the one having to wait.
I don't mind
that you have to wait
but I don't want to have to
wait with you.
I hate to wait
because
I tend to put myself
in the one place
I am never supposed to be
and
I tend to want to be
the one thing
I should never crave to be.
I hate to wait because
I want to be
in the center of my universe
and I want to be
my own sovereign.
When I forget Your plan
When I lose sight of Your will
When I begin to think
that my life belongs to me
When I fall prey to
the delusion
that I am wiser than You
and
my way is better than Yours
Then I hate to wait
and
I curse the obstacles in my way.
But You are sovereign
and You are
Good
and loving
and gracious

and kind
and mighty,
filled with compassion
overflowing with mercy.
You bought me
with the price of Your Son.
You forgave me
and the cost was His death.
For all my attempts
at independent wisdom
and
self-sovereignty
the truth is
that my life does not belong to me.
So
once more I fall to my knees.
Once more I open my hands
and
give my life back to You
and say,
"You do in, with, and through me
what You think is best
and
I will follow
and when
Your wisdom and grace
require it,
I will be willing
to wait."

Take a Moment

1. Is there an area in your life in which you are fighting the fact that God has chosen to grace you with waiting?
2. What does your struggle with waiting reveal about your heart and about what is truly important to you?

37 | Losing Heart

> Wait for the LORD;
> be strong, and let your heart take courage;
> wait for the LORD!
>
> PSALM 27:14

What causes a person to lose heart? What makes a person want to give up? Why do we ever entertain fantasies of running away? What causes us to have little enthusiasm for what we once found very motivating?

Your motivation to continue is only as strong as what you have placed your hope in. Perhaps this is why we so easily lose heart in the face of obstacles, opposition, or difficulty. Perhaps what we have unwittingly done is try to build our reason for continuing on the shifting sand of flawed and impermanent things that were never meant to be the foundation of our meaning and purpose or our inner sense of well-being.

No human being is capable of carrying your hope. This side of heaven we are all weak and flawed in some way. No circumstance can carry your hope. Every situation you are in is in some way touched by the brokenness of the fall and isn't under your control. Amassing physical pleasures and possessions won't give you lasting hope. For all of their momentary enjoyment, they fill the senses but do not satisfy the heart. When you look horizontally for your reason to continue you will inevitably end up losing hope.

This is precisely why you could hear no better advice than that found in the three words that begin and end the last verse of Psalm 27, "Wait for the LORD." What are you waiting for? Are you waiting for your husband to finally become romantic? Are you waiting for your wife to finally agree that your marriage isn't so bad after all? Are you waiting for that job that will fulfill you? Are you waiting for life to get easier? Are you waiting for your church to finally become all a church could be? Where do you look and say, "If only I had_______ then my life would be________"?

There is only one place where stable and reliable hope can be found. There is only one place of rest for your heart and surety for your soul. There is only one reliable place to find your reason to get up in the morning and continue. There is only one source of motivation that is sturdy enough to weather the storms of life in a fallen world. "Wait for the LORD" really does say it all.

When your hope is in the Lord, when you are getting your inner sense of well-being and security from him, when he is the reason you continue even when things are hard, then you are building your life on something that is reliable and sure. When you are waiting on the Lord, you have placed your hope in one who is the ultimate source of everything that's wise, good, and true. When you wait for the Lord, you are placing your safety in the hands of one whose power is immeasurable. When you wait for the Lord, you are getting your comfort from one whose love is boundless. When you wait for the Lord, you can be secure in the reality that he rules over all things. When you wait for the Lord, you can live with confidence because you know that every one of his promises is true. When you wait for the Lord, you can be hopeful even in weakness because you know that his grace is sufficient.

We lose heart because we tie our hope to the wrong things. What are you waiting for? To what have you tied your hope? "Be strong and let your heart take courage; wait for the LORD."

Take a Moment

1. Where is your hope disappointing you because it is simply the wrong hope? Hope in what thing or person tends to compete with your hope in the Lord?

2. How would your daily living change if you were responding to the situations and relationships of your life from a heart filled with hope in the Lord?

38 | Where You Gonna Run, Where You Gonna Hide?

> The LORD is the stronghold of my life;
> of whom shall I be afraid?
>
> PSALM 27:16b

We all look for a place to hide. We all have places where we run. We all search for shelter. We do this because we have all experienced, at various times and in many different ways, the danger of life in a fallen world. This world, broken by sin, really is a dangerous place.

There is the danger of being sinned against. Most of our experience of being sinned against takes place in the mundane little moments of everyday life. Maybe you are nursing the wounds from something someone said to you. Maybe you are dealing with the hurt of what someone did to you. These are not really big things, but they unsettle you and make you wonder whom you can trust.

But being sinned against isn't always so mundane. Perhaps you have been hospitalized from injuries from a mugging. Maybe you are dealing with the devastation of an unfaithful spouse. Maybe you have lost your job as the result of the lies of someone who envied your position. There is no way of matriculating through this fallen world without being sinned against by someone at some time.

There is the danger of living in a world that doesn't operate as was intended. We live in a world where things like racism, materialism, corrupt government, and war alter the lives of many. We live in a world where disease and pollution are virtually inescapable. We live in a world where earthquakes, hurricanes, and tsunamis are present realities. The brokenness of the environment in which we live touches us all.

There is the danger of temptation and spiritual warfare. You and I really do live in a world where an Evil One exists. There really is a cosmic battle going on. There is an enemy who wants to plant deceit, division, destruction, and death anywhere he can. You and I have never experienced even one day that has been free of seductive lies being whispered in our ears and seductive visions being held before our eyes. Temptation assaults all around and wears us down; such is life in the fallen world.

There is the danger that you are to yourself. Sin reduces all of us to fools. It makes right look wrong to us and wrong look right. It makes us want to live more for the moment than for long-term gain. Sin makes us self-absorbed and self-focused. It causes us to be self-excusing and self-atoning. It makes us defensive and self-protective. It causes us to opt for individuality rather than community. The danger of the fallen world isn't only around us; it's inside us as well.

So, when you have been wounded by the dangers of this broken world, where do you run to for refuge? When you are perceptive enough to see the danger coming, where do you run to for protection? When you are exhausted with the difficulty of the journey, where do you turn for rest and retreat? Do you run to other people, hoping that they will be your personal messiah? Do you run to food, numbing your mind with the edible glories of creation? Do you run to YouTube or your iPod, hoping to distract yourself out of your pain? Do you drink more than you should or bury yourself in busyness?

The problem is that these things were never designed to be a place of refuge for you. When you seek these things as your shelter, you will always be disappointed because their solace is temporary and they have no ability to heal the soul. But there is another thing: they always end up addicting you and, in so doing, hurt you as well. Take food, for instance. It gives me very quickly diminishing comfort, so I soon need more. You can see how co-opting food for comfort can end in a cycle of addiction.

You're gonna run, and you're gonna hide. Here is what you need to understand: there is only one true place of shelter. The Lord really is the world's only reliable stronghold. He has the power to protect you, and he has the grace to restore your soul. He gives strength to the weary and returns the joy of the broken. He is able to renew you, body and soul. Heaven and earth obey his commands. He is the shelter of shelters, the only safe place to hide. He delights in holding you in the hollow of his hand. He takes joy in covering you in the shadow of his wing.

Today you will run to something. Today you will hide somewhere. Why not, this time, run to the Lord?

Take a Moment

1. When you're in danger or feeling discouraged, where do you tend to run?
2. Where, right now, in the troubles of life, does your soul need rest? What would it look like to find it in the Lord?

39 | Days of Beauty

One thing have I asked of the LORD,
    that will I seek after:
that I may dwell in the house of the LORD
    all the days of my life,
to gaze upon the beauty of the LORD
    and to inquire in his temple.

PSALM 27:4

I have a vision problem;
my eyes are okay,
but my heart
doesn't see very well.
I live in a world
where Your beauty
is everywhere visible.
It is there
in the lily.
It is there
in the cascading wave.
It is there
in the multi-hued sunset.
It is there
in the stars of the night.
It is there
in the power of the storm.
It is there
in the rhythm of the rain.
It is there
in the grandeur of the mountain.
It is there
in the lace of the clouds.
It is there
in the succulence of the apple.
It is there

everywhere I look.
But often
I do not see Your beauty.
I must confess
I am so blind.
I see
my busy schedule.
I see
things to be fixed.
I see
obstacles to my plan.
I see
bills to be paid.
I see
things to be done.
I see,
but I fail to see Your beauty.
Yet there is more:
I call things beautiful
that are not beautiful to You.
I am attracted to things
that You call ugly.
I even begin to believe
that there are things
more beautiful
than You.
And I want these things more
than You.
So I serve these things more
than You.
So, Lord
correct my vision.
Please restore
the eyes of my heart.
Graciously make
the days that I have left
to be
days of beauty
because my heart
is filled
with visions of You.

Take a Moment

1. Where is God's beauty on visible display for you day after day?
2. What thing in your life blinds you to the display of divine beauty that is everywhere around you?

40 | Going to School

Teach me your way, O LORD,
and lead me on a level path
because of my enemies.
PSALM 27:11

So who is schooling you? There is never a day that passes without your being taken to school in some way. Life is really all about teaching and learning. And there is a way in which neither stops from the first day until the last day of your life. So, perhaps one of the most important diagnostic questions that each of us should be asking is this: "Do I approach life as a student?"

If you are committed to know and understand, if you are committed to journey from ignorance to knowledge and from foolishness to wisdom, if you are interested in more than your own plan and perspective, then it only makes sense to learn at the feet of the world's best Teacher. Who could know more or be wiser than the One who put the universe into motion, who presently holds it together, and who controls its destiny? Who could know more about the true meaning and purpose of life? Who could know more about your identity? Who could know more about the environment in which you live? Who could know more about the foundational questions of life?

The Proverbs say it very well: "The fear of the LORD is the beginning of wisdom." I like John Calvin's paraphrase of that: "There is no knowing that does not begin with knowing God." There can be no better place to go to school than to the University of the Lord and there could be no better course of study than the way of the Lord.

His way is wisdom, and wisdom requires understanding his way. So where are you going for wisdom? Whose school have you been attending? Who shapes your definition of the meaning and purpose of life? Who tells you who you are and what you should be doing?

Who crafts the way you look at the surrounding world? Who defines your problems? Who instructs you as to how they will be solved? Who helps you to determine your life's direction? Who tells you what is functionally important and what isn't? Who shapes your relationships? Who clarifies your thinking in moments of difficulty? Are you really a faithful student in the school of the Lord, or do you just audit now and then when it's convenient? Let me suggest the characteristics of a student in the school of the Lord.

A healthy cynicism toward your own wisdom. Sin reduces all of us to fools, but it does something else that is even more insidious: it makes us believe that we are wise. Independent wisdom was both the seductive temptation and the delusional desire behind the fall. One of the primary reasons Adam and Eve were attracted to the fruit was that it was "to be desired to make one wise." But eating the fruit didn't result in wisdom; no, it opened the floodgates of foolishness, and we have been drowning in its waters ever since.

You and I were never created with the autonomous capacity to be wise. Wisdom doesn't come through research, experience, and study. Wisdom comes by revelation and relationship. You only get wisdom from the One who is its ultimate source, the Lord.

A humble sense of need. We all get lulled to sleep by feelings of arrival, by feeling satisfied with our character, our knowledge, and our behavior. We have little desire for further growth. You know what it's like. We all have the capacity to be too easily satisfied. Because we know more today than we did yesterday, we quit working to know more tomorrow. Rather than gratitude for what God has taught us, motivating us to learn more, we get smug and lazy, quite content to consider ourselves God's graduates.

A willing and open heart. Willingness and openness are the essential characteristics of any good student. Why, you may ask? Because learning not only shows me what I didn't know, but it points out the places where what I thought I knew was, in fact, wrong. I cannot tell you how many defensive students I have met in my many years of teaching. "Defensive student" is actually an oxymoron, like jumbo shrimp or low-fat butter. You can't be defensive and be a student. You have to open up your heart. You have to be willing to be told that you are wrong. You have to submit yourself to someone who knows better and knows more. Defending what you know won't lead to either further or corrected understanding. Willingness to listen, consider, and change are in the heart of every good student.

Discernment, focus, and determination. Discernment means that you have to make sure you are submitting yourself to qualified teachers. Paul says in Colossians 2:8: "See to it that no one takes you captive by philosophy and empty deceit, according to human tradition, according to the elemental spirits of the world, and not according to Christ." Once you are sitting at the feet of those who represent the Teacher of teachers, then continued learning takes focus.

You live in a world of many, many voices. All of them are interpreting your world and all of them are vying for the allegiance of your heart. And you have to remember that learning is a process, not an event. One truth opens the doorway to another truth. One truth functions as an interpreter of a truth previously introduced but now understood more fully. Learning is a lifelong process, and because it is, it requires perseverance.

Commitment to act on what you are learning. Any seasoned teacher will tell you that the real learning takes place after the students leave the classroom and practice what they have been taught. The God who is your teacher will orchestrate events, situations, and relationships for the purpose of causing you to live what you have been learning. Life is his classroom, and in every new location on each new day, provides a rich and God-given environment to understand more deeply and to live more wisely. So, good students always carry with them the commitment to look for ways to apply what they have been learning, and they know that as they do, their learning will continue.

By God's grace we haven't been left to our own wisdom. We have been brought into personal communion with the One who is the source of everything that's wise and true. So these questions remain: Are you a committed student? Whose school are you attending?

Take a Moment

1. Is God calling you, in the way that you approach life, to live with more of the character of a student?
2. Where do you tend to turn for the wisdom needed to deal with what is on your plate?

41 | The Good Life

> I believe that I shall look upon the goodness of the LORD in the land of the living!
>
> PSALM 27:13

If you could paint a portrait of your version of the good life, what would it look like? What's the golden personal dream that fills your mind when you say to yourself, "If only I had . . ."? What's the one thing in your life that you tell yourself would make you happy?

It is very tempting to associate the good life with something physical. Perhaps, for you, it would mean living in a certain location. Maybe it would mean getting that job that you've always dreamed of. Or it could mean having the special relationship with that special person. Maybe, for you, it would be earning a certain amount of money. Maybe it would be looking a certain way or experiencing a certain level of physical health.

When you define the good life by these kinds of physical experiences there is a second thing that happens: you tend to judge God by his willingness to deliver them to you. You unwittingly begin to evaluate God's goodness by whether he gives you the thing that you have set your heart on. But often God doesn't give us the things that we have set our hearts on, precisely because we have set our hearts on them. Because we have set our hearts on them they are a spiritual danger to us. So God is responding to us in a way that's good, even though it doesn't feel good at the moment. It's often in these moments of want that we are experiencing the "goodness of the LORD in the land of the living." Because he loves us and because he's good, God keeps from us those things that fight for control of our hearts and, therefore, fight for the place that only he is supposed to have.

Imagine a little child running to the house one afternoon and saying to his mom, "Mommy, I am hungry. I want a candy bar, a can of soda, and a bowl of ice cream." The mother responds, "I'll make you a peanut butter sandwich with some apple slices on the side." There's a good possibility that your child won't run over to his friend's house and say, "You won't believe what a good mom I have. I asked for unhealthy treats, and she responded by giving me things that were much better." The more likely scenario is that the child would immediately protest to his mother, "I don't want peanut butter! I want candy. Why can't I have candy?" At this moment your child doesn't think of you as the definition of parental goodness!

Being confident of the goodness of the Lord shouldn't be confused with an assumption that because God is good, he will give me the things that I've set my heart on. In his grace, God is freeing you from the small confines of your little definition of what is good so that you can experience the huge and satisfying good that he has planned for you. Grace welcomes me to experience what is eternally right, true, and good. Grace invites me to good that I could never have imagined, deserved, or earned.

It's nice to have a beautiful house and a comfortable life, but it's even better to come to the place where you no longer need those things to feel good about your life. Sure God will bless me with physical things, but every good physical thing that he gives me is meant to be a sign that points me to the good that can be found only in him.

This is the bottom line. The good that God promises me isn't a situation, possession, position, or relationship. The good that he promises me is himself. What could possibly be a better gift than that?

Take a Moment

1. Be honest—if you could paint a portrait of your personal definition of the good life, what would it look like?
2. Are you tempted to replace joy in God's gift of himself with some physical possession, experience, or relationship?

42 | Family Forever

> For my father and my mother have forsaken me,
> but the LORD will take me in.
>
> PSALM 27:10

I deserve to be
forsaken
to be forever cast away.
I deserve to be
rejected
to have You turn away and stay.
I have debated Your goodness.
I have questioned Your law.
I have doubted Your wisdom.
I have run from Your love.
I deserve Your
anger
to be punished for my wrong.
I deserve Your
righteous judgment
the full weight of Your law.
I have wanted what I wanted.
I've walked from Your grace.
I have trespassed Your boundaries.
I have envied Your throne.
I don't deserve Your
affection,
the many things I could not earn.
I don't deserve Your
provision,
the daily gifts of Your love.
I don't deserve the rights of
family,
to be called Your son.

I don't deserve the warm
reception,
Tender care and endless help.
I don't deserve to call You
Father
to be welcomed in Your home.
So You came to be
rejected,
to have the Father turn His face.
Your bond of family was
broken
You came to stand in my place.
You didn't deserve to be
rejected
It came because of Your love.
You didn't deserve to be
forsaken
yet You were willing to the end.
So now I have a
family,
Forever I've been received.
I am never
forsaken
Even when I'm all alone.
When fatherless and
friendless,
You are with me even then.
I have been given a
family
I did not deserve or earn.
The Lord has
received me.
I will never be alone.
Once more I will forsake You.
I will question Your love.
Once more I will debate You.
I will turn from Your face.
But You will come as a
Father.
You will treat me as a son.
You will forgive and
restore me.

With great patience and great love.
In You I've found a
family.
In You I have found grace.
And what I've found, I've found
forever.
Forever Father.
Forever family.
Forever welcomed.
Forever love.

Take a Moment

1. Do you live with the courage and hope that comes from knowing that you are never alone?
2. Is there a person whom you tend to look to for the security of the unfailing love and acceptance that you have already been given by your heavenly Father?

43 | Caught in the Middle

> Wait for the LORD;
> be strong, and let your heart take courage;
> wait for the LORD!
>
> PSALM 27:14

We spend a lot of our lives "caught in the middle." We head to work and get caught in the middle of a traffic jam. We enter a conversation and get caught in the middle of an argument. We make an investment and get caught in the middle of a market downturn. We join a church and get caught in the middle of a theological controversy. We dream of our future and get caught in the middle of things we did not foresee and would not have chosen. We really do spend much of our time caught in the middle of being caught in the middle.

When you are required to wait, it means that you are caught in the middle of something, and when you are caught in the middle of something, it immediately means that you are part of something bigger than you. Being caught in the middle is disconcerting and irritating because we all tend to give into the delusion that we have more power and control over our lives than we actually have.

Self-sovereignty is the dream of every sinner. It's hard for us to trust ourselves to the wisdom, power, and control of another. We want to write our own dramas, and we want to be the central character of the story. But the spiritual reality of the universe is that we are not the authors of our own story. Our story is a part of a larger story that is written by the Lord. In this story we are never on center stage. That is a position to be occupied by the Lord alone.

When you recognize that you are caught in the middle of something, you are recognizing something that is profoundly important. Let me detail how practically important this insight is.

First, it means you were meant to live for something bigger than yourself. You are not in control. Your story is not ultimate. You have been created to be part of something that is larger than your wants, your needs, and your feelings. You are connected to something that is bigger than your relationships, your situations, and the locations that you move in every day. You are waiting, because God said you are a part of his kingdom. God, whose timing is always perfect, works according to his wise plan and at the right moment. But as you wait, he is doing something in and for you. He is crafting you into the person his grace alone enables you to be.

Second, it means you were created to be dependent. The independent, this-is-my-life-and-this-is-what-I-will-do-with-it view is a delusion. The thought that you have everything you need to be what you are supposed to be and to do what you are supposed to do is a fantasy. Each of us is dependent on God for our physical life. We all know that we do not control the many, many things around us that must work in order for our lives to work. We all know that our life doesn't work according to our plan. We couldn't write the story of today and accurately predict what we will face. Contrary to what we often think and how we often act, we all live a life of reliance on God.

Third, it means that the things you need most you cannot provide for yourself. God has controlled the forces of nature and the events of human history in order to give me the one thing I desperately need and could never earn, deserve, or achieve—new birth. Without the intervention of his powerful heart and life and his transforming grace, I would be a dead man walking. But he has given me life, and he is now working to change me into what I, if left to myself, could never be. I wait because his grace is still at work. I wait because he is not done and I am not yet complete.

Fourth, it means the final chapter of your story has been written but has not yet unfolded. There are more places God has written for me. There are more characters to appear in my story. There are circumstances that he has designed for me to encounter. There are moments of blessing and times of difficulty that have already been written into my story by the One who is not only in control but is also wise, gracious, kind, and good. He already knows the exact path he will cause me to walk and how that path will result in his glory and my good. I could never write an autobiography that would accomplish what his story for me already has and will accomplish.

Fifth, it means that the One you are waiting for is trustworthy. I know that there are times when waiting is painful. I know there are times when it seems as if it is impossible to wait. But you and I must remind ourselves that we wait not because irrational and impersonal forces function as obstructions and interferences in our lives. No, we wait because the world is carefully administered by the one Person who is ultimate in power, ultimate in authority, and ultimate in wisdom, while at the very same time being ultimate in love. You are being asked to wait by One you can trust.

Sixth, it means that in those moments when you are caught, you can rest. Don't give way to panic. Don't give into doubt because this is not what you would have planned. Don't allow yourself to play out all of the "what if's" and "if only's" in your mind. You are waiting because there is a plan. You are waiting because your life is under the control of One who is wise and good. You can rest, not because you know what is happening, but because you know the One who is in control of what is happening to you right now. You can rest because you know he has made you a part of something wonderful, and he knows what he is doing in you is good, even though at this moment it feels as if you have been caught in the middle.

Take a Moment

1. In what area of your life do you tend to be frustrated and irritated because you are "caught in the middle?"
2. How would your living change if you embraced the reality that God has already written a better story for you than you could have ever written for yourself?

44 | From Your Lips to Messiah's Ears

> I will offer in his tent
> sacrifices with shouts of joy.
>
> PSALM 27:6

My son Darnay and I were fortunate enough to get tickets for an NBA playoff game. The local home team, the Philadelphia 76ers, was playing its rival the Boston Celtics. I had never before and never after did I experienced the noise of that night.

As we entered the arena, the air was already alive with anticipation. People were high-fiving one another before the game started, just because they were excited to be in the building! The volume began to crank up as the teams were introduced and continued to build as the game progressed. The fires of enthusiasm were stoked by the closeness of the game and the historical rivalry of the two teams. By the third quarter the entire crowd was on its feet doing what could only be characterized as screaming at the top of their lungs. I tried to make an observation to Darnay, but he could not hear me. I tried again, only to have us break into laughter at the impossibility of communicating and the complete frenzy of the crowd.

I remember walking to the car and thinking about the event. I couldn't think of another time when I had shouted so loud for so long, and I realized my ears were ringing from the audio stress I had just put them through.

What makes you shout? We all do it. Sometimes it is a response of complete surprise. Sometimes it is the result of sheer delight. Sometimes it is a way to get attention. Sometimes it is the reflex of fear. Sometimes it is the product of anger. Sometimes it is the anguish of disappointment. Sometimes it is verbalizing pain. Sometimes it is the welling up of a grateful heart. Whom do you shout at, and what do you shout for? Where do you want your shouting to go—from your lips, to whose ears? The point is that in your life there are things that make you shout, and what makes you shout reveals something about what is going on in your heart.

Now, let me make what at first may seem like a weird connection for you. There is a direct connection between shouting and worship. Before you think I'm crazy, let me explain my statement. *Worship* is a tricky word. It conjures up in our minds all kinds of formal ritualistic religious images. But worship, in its most basic biblical usage, is an identity that shapes activity. You are a worshiper, which is why you worship. What does it mean to be a worshiper? It means that you are a purpose-driven or value-driven being. There is something always laying claim to the rulership of your heart. There is something for which you are living. There is something of value that gives shape to why you do what you do and say what you say in the situations and relationships of your daily life. There is something you look to for identity, meaning and purpose, and an inner sense of well-being.

Now let me make the connection between shouting and worship more practical. If I am a salesman who lives for the affluent life that successful sales calls provide, and if I get my identity from the big house and luxury car that those sales make possible, then I will shout in anger when traffic keeps me from a potential sale. I am not actually mad at the traffic; I am mad because the traffic is in the way of what gives me value. I will also shout for joy when I read the e-mail that informs me that the last call resulted in the biggest single sale of my career.

Shouting really does reveal what is important to you. If you are a parent, listen for what makes you shout. If you are a worker, listen for what makes you shout. If you are one of God's children, listen for what makes you shout. If you are married, listen for what makes you shout. Listen and consider what is really important to you. When the thing that is my true treasure in life is taken out of my hands, I will shout in dismay, and when it is placed in my hands, I will shout for joy. Shouting really does reveal what has come to rule your heart.

That is what makes this part of Psalm 27 so remarkable. David says that when he makes sacrifices he shouts for joy. In so doing

David reveals what is really important to him. It is important to him to admit who he is. Sacrifice is only necessary in the life of a sinner. So, when David says he sacrifices with shouts of joy, he is humbly embracing the reality of how deep and consistent his problem with sin actually is. You will only ever be excited with the sacrifice that brings forgiveness when you find comfort in admitting who you really are.

But there is more. David sacrifices with shouts of joy because he is utterly amazed that a righteous God, who is repulsed by sin, would graciously make a way for him to be forgiven. Could there be a more needful and glorious reason to shout than the fact that in this broken world, populated by lost, flawed, and rebellious people, real forgiveness is possible? What could bring you more joy than to realize that you can stand completely exposed before God, without even a hint of fear, because a sacrifice has been made that has paid your penalty and granted your forgiveness?

Without knowing it, David was shouting to Jesus as he made his sacrifice. All the sacrifices of the old covenant looked to that sacrifice that was to come when the Messiah, the Shepherd Lamb, would suffer cruel torture and be hung as a criminal, so that all who put their trust in him would be fully and completely forgiven.

Yes, you shout, if even under your breath. And, yes, your shouting reveals something about what is important to you. When has the reality of your forgiveness last caused you to shout for joy? When have you been so filled with gratitude that you wanted your joy to go from your lips to the Messiah's ears?

Take a Moment

1. What do your shouts of joy and grief reveal about the true treasures of your heart?
2. What shouts of thanksgiving need to be in your heart as you remember that no matter what you are called to face, you face it as a recipient of the forgiving, empowering, and transforming grace of God?

45 | Why Bother?

> I believe that I shall look upon the goodness of the LORD in the land of the living!
> PSALM 27:13

I consider
the brokenness of the world
and I think,
"Why bother?"
I look
at the corruption all around me
and I cry,
"Why bother?"
I wonder at
my inability to live with my neighbor
and I ask,
"Why bother?"
I face
my war with sin inside and outside,
and I ponder,
"Why bother?"
I look
at the problems of the culture around me
and I lament,
"Why bother?"
I scan
my world, broken by disease and misuse,
and in sadness say,
"Why bother?"
I consider
the statistics of violence and abuse
and I think,
"Why bother?"
I am assaulted

with the reality of endless wars between nations,
and overwhelmed say,
"Why wonder?"
I am defeated
by temptation's power
and cry,
"Why bother?"
I ponder
how good is called bad and bad good,
and in frustration say,
"Why bother?"
I search
for hope like a parched man for water
but end up thinking,
"Why bother?"
I look
to myself and see weakness and want,
and in grief say,
"Why bother?"
Perhaps
I should live for leisure and comfort
and give into
"Why bother?"
Maybe
I should exist for the here and now,
and forgetting forever say,
"Why bother?"
I am tempted
to live for power and control,
and for greater things say,
"Why bother?"
Perhaps
personal pleasure in the here and now
is what it's all about;
"Why bother?"
But in
exhaustion I look up and not around
and I say,
"Why bother?"

Why bother?
Because You are and You are good.

Why bother?
Because You dispense goodness and grace.
Why bother?
Because You bring life out of death.
Why bother?
Because You have a plan and it will be done.
Why bother?
Because I have been welcomed into Your Kingdom of Life.
Why bother?
Because I am always with You.

It is true
that my eyes don't always see
and my heart isn't always confident.
It is true that darkness overwhelms me
and fear leaves me weak.
But You come near.
You remind me once again
that I can be confident
because
You were unwilling to say,
"Why bother?"

Take a Moment

1. Is there a place right now where you are wondering if it is worth it to continue?
2. What specific truths will give you reason to continue as you face the disappointments and difficulties of life?

46 | Productive Delay

> Wait for the LORD;
> be strong, and let your heart take courage;
> wait for the LORD!
>
> PSALM 27:14

For years I just didn't get the biblical concept of waiting. Waiting seemed a meaningless drag, forced onto us by the fact that Someone else is in charge of the narrative that is our lives. We hope, we dream, and we wait. We cry, we plead, and we wait. We run, we work, and we wait. We minister, we serve, and we wait. We think, we study, and we wait. Sometimes we wait, we wait, and we wait. Such is life in the middle of God's great, big redemptive story. So, with gritted teeth and emotions that fall short of joy, we resolve ourselves to the fact that we'll have to wait. God is God and we are not; so what can we do? We wait.

I guess my concept of waiting was along the lines of what I experience in the dentist's office. My appointment has been scheduled for 10:00 AM, but I know that I won't be seen until 10:45. I'm already uptight at the time I'll waste, sitting in that office with nothing to do. I sat recently in a physician's office waiting room with a sign that read, "No cell phones please!"

So you look for some way to make the mind-numbing minutes go by. But what seems to be hours, by a quick glance at your watch, proves to have been only six minutes.

To pass the time, we pick up magazines that we wouldn't normally choose to read. You know you're a man who has been in the dentist's office too long when you find yourself reading *Ladies' Home Journal* and thinking that the ingredients in the recipe that you're looking at actually seem quite tasty. You are tempted to tear it out and take it home with you! You want to call your wife and say, "Dear, I've found the best recipe for chicken," when suddenly you think, "What am I doing?"

But waiting on God isn't like this at all. Waiting on God isn't about the suspension of meaning and purpose. It's part of the meaning and purpose that God has brought into my life. Waiting on God isn't to be viewed as an obstruction in the way of the plan. Waiting is an essential part of the plan. For the child of God, waiting isn't simply about what the child will receive at the end of his wait. No, waiting is much more purposeful, efficient, and practical. Waiting is fundamentally about what we will become as we wait.

God is using the wait to do in and through me exactly what he has promised. Through the wait he is changing me. By means of the wait he is altering the fabric of my thoughts and desires. Through the wait he is causing me to see and experience new things about him and his kingdom. And all of this sharpens me, enabling me to be a more useful tool in his redemptive hands.

Waiting on God is restorative. It is one of the tools God uses to remake us into what we were designed to be in the beginning. Yet I don't like to wait, and I still struggle to wait well. How about you? The next time God calls you to wait, don't let your mind go to the dentist's office. Picture in your mind the nimble and skilled fingers of a potter who is putting pressure on the clay right where it's needed so that it will take on the beauty that is its potential. And with this picture in mind, give thanks for the very moment that once would have driven you crazy.

Take a Moment

1. In what area of your life is God causing you to wait in order to restore you to what he created you to be?
2. How are you responding to waiting? What would change if you responded to waiting by believing that it really is spiritually beneficial to you?

47 | Hearts at Rest

> Though an army encamp against me,
> my heart shall not fear.
>
> PSALM 27:3

I would like to say
that
my heart is at rest,
but I can't.
I would like to think
that
I always rest in God's care,
but I don't.
I would love to declare
that
my faith is unwavering,
but it isn't.
I wish it was a fact
that
fear is a thing of my past,
but it simply isn't.
It would be nice to know
that
trust's struggle is over,
but it isn't.
I wish I never wanted
to be
my own sovereign,
but I do.
I want to have unbroken rest
in
the hand of God's love,
but I don't.
I long to face difficulty

without
question or doubt,
but I don't.
I do not want to
re-question
my Father's love,
but I do.
I wish I never questioned
the
Lord's good plan,
but I do.
The struggle is better
than
it once was,
but not done.
My rest is more consistent
than
it used to be,
but not complete.
My heart enjoys a greater ease
than
in earlier days of faith,
but unrest comes.
I have lived with You
and
seen Your care,
but questions come.
I have seen You do
what
I could not have conceived,
but still doubt.
I have been in awe
of
the provisions of Your grace,
but anxiety comes.
I have submitted myself
to
Your will and way,
but still rebel.
So with rest in Your forgiveness
and
confidence in Your power,

I come.
With a needy heart
that
craves Your help,
I pray:
"Help me, Father, today
to
let go of my need
to always understand.
Enable me to live in rest
when
I don't know before
what will happen.
Help me to have a restful heart
when
opposition is great,
and all I have is You."

Take a Moment

1. Is there evidence from the way you live that your heart is not at rest?
2. Where are you demanding understanding rather than resting in God, who is faithful, loving, wise, powerful, and good?

48 | False Witnesses

> Give me not up to the will of my adversaries;
> for false witnesses have risen against me,
> and they breathe out violence.
>
> PSALM 27:12

It really does hurt when you are falsely accused. It is painful to think that someone is convinced that you did something that you didn't do. It is frustrating to be accused of a wrong you had nothing to do with. It is maddening when you seem unable to do anything to explain or defend yourself.

All of us have experienced it. We play the accusation over and over in the DVD player in our brain. We rewind the accusatory conversation. We wonder what people think about us, haunted by the soiled reputation we are convinced that we will now carry around. We look for ways to justify ourselves. We search for things we can say and do to restore our reputation. It is painful to be innocent yet unable to live with the charges that have been made against us.

Your Lord and Savior, Jesus Christ, was in that place, but he put himself there on purpose. Confused? Let me explain. Jesus came to earth knowing exactly what he was going to be facing. He came as an act of submission to the Father's great redemptive plan (see John 6:38). He came with a willing spirit, willing to face the very things that we all work to avoid and find so painful when they are unavoidable. Passages like Isaiah 53 and these verses in Psalm 27 give us a window into the depth of the love of Christ.

It is almost impossible to conceive that the King of kings, the great Creator, the sovereign Son of God would submit to this:

> He would submit to being betrayed by a close friend.
> He would submit to being led away toward a wrongful trial.

He would submit to being forsaken by his closest followers.
He would submit to false accusations.
He would submit to gross injustice.
He would stand silent while being mocked.
He would submit to slaps on the face.
He would not defend himself against physical torture.
He would submit to a mob that would call for his death.
He would submit to the pain of a crown of thorns.
He would be willing to drag his cross to the place of his execution.
He would submit to being identified with criminals.
He would submit to nails being driven into his limbs.
He would be willing to have his Father turn his back on him.

Yes, he knew the cruelties and injustices that he would face. And he was willing. In that final moment before he faced the unthinkable, Jesus prayed something very similar to Psalm 27:12. He prayed, "Father, if it be possible, let this cup pass from me . . ." (Matt. 26:39); in other words, "Do not turn me over to the desire of my foes." But then he added these words of amazing submission, words that made our salvation possible: ". . . not as I will, but as you will."

Jesus knew the plan. From the first moment of his life on earth, he knew that he was marching toward that moment when he would be turned over to the desire of his foes. He knew false witnesses would seal his death. He knew, but they did not. They didn't know that they weren't in charge. They didn't know that they were part of a greater plan. They had no idea that, long before they were born, God had chosen to turn their moment of deceit and injustice into a moment of triumph and salvation.

He knew false witnesses were in his future; he is the Savior, and he was willing.

Take a Moment

1. Are there places in your life where you tend to feel that you are alone and that your trouble is unique?

2. Read Hebrews 4:14–5:3 and thank Jesus that he was willing to suffer what you and I suffer so that he would be able to offer us grace that is appropriate to our time of need.

49 | A Plan for Your Life

> . . . That I may dwell in the house of the LORD
> all the days of my life,
> to gaze upon the beauty of the LORD
> and to inquire in his temple.
>
> PSALM 27:4

Now, admit it—you love yourself, and you have a wonderful plan for your life. Somehow, someway we all are too focused on our own lives. All of us get captured by what we want, what we feel, and what we have determined we need. Every one of us is a dreamer. We have all been given the amazing capacity to envision the future and to plan toward it. A dream is imagination coupled with desire and projected into the future. There are things that you would love to have as part of your life. There are things that you would like to accomplish. There are locations you would love to experience. There are relationships you would like to enjoy. There are situations you would like to avoid. Every day you get up and you work toward some kind of dream.

But dreamers don't just dream their dream; they also dream to be sovereign. In some way, at some time, all of us have wished that we had enough control over our lives to guarantee that we could experience the things we have dreamed. We would like to control people and situations just enough to ensure that the "good things" we've dreamed would actually come true. What does the Bible call all of this? The Bible calls it worship.

You see, you and I are worshipers. This is one of the things that separates us from the rest of creation. As worshipers we are always living for something. Something is always laying claim to the affection and rulership of our hearts. There is always something that commands our dreams. There is something that we look to for identity, meaning, and purpose, and that inner sense of well-being that everyone seeks.

Scripture says that there are only two choices (Rom. 1:25). Either you are living in pursuit of the creation or you are living in pursuit of the Creator. You are looking for your satisfaction and meaning in the physical, created world, or you are finding it in the Lord.

This means that there is a war of dreams that rages in our hearts, and in the middle of the fog of this war it is so easy to get it wrong. It is so easy to think that because we have our theology in the right place, because we are biblically literate and functioning members of a good church, that our lives are shaped by worship of the Lord. But that may not be the case at all. On closer inspection, it may actually be the case that underneath all of those things we are driven by personal success, or material things, or the respect of others, or power and control. I am deeply persuaded that there's a whole lot of idolatrous Christianity out there. The most dangerous idols are those that fit well within the culture of external Christianity.

It's here that Psalm 27 is so helpful and convicting. What is David's dream for his life? What is his plan? Well, the answer sounds so spiritual as to be impractical, but it gets right to the heart of why we were created in the first place. David says, in Old Testament language, "I want to spend my life in worship of the Lord. I want to dwell in his temple and gaze upon his beauty." The shekinah-glory presence of the Lord filled the holy place of the temple, like a cloud. It was a physical picture of God dwelling with his people. David was saying, "I want to be where God is. I want to do what I was created to do."

No, David isn't some super-spiritual mystic. David gets it right. His quest is for a life shaped and directed by a daily worship of the Lord. David knows who he is: a creature created for worship. David knows who God is: the only "thing" in the universe truly worthy of worship. His dream is the best dream that you could ever dream. Far from being impractical, this dream, if lived out at street level, will bring purity and peace to your life.

What is your plan for your life? How close is your plan to the plan God had for you when he gave you life and breath? Is there, perhaps, something in your plan that competes for the place that only God should have?

May your plan for you be identical to his plan for you!

Take a Moment

1. How close is your dream for your life to the plan for life to which God has called you?
2. Is God calling you to let go of a dream so that his plan for you may flourish?

50 | Stumbling at the Cross

When evil men advance against me
to devour my flesh,
when my enemies and my foes attack me,
they will stumble and fall.
PSALM 27:2 (NIV)

What do the Psalms look to? What is the theme that courses its way through psalm after psalm? What gives the Psalms their meaning and depth? The thing that the Psalms point to again and again isn't a "thing" at all. No, it's a person, and his name is Jesus. It's not as though some of the psalms are Messianic; all of the psalms point to the person and work of the Savior in some way! Psalm 27 is a powerful example.

You can't help but think of the cross when you read the words of Psalm 27:2. There was a dramatic moment in time when evil men advanced against Christ. It was a moment of jealous injustice. It seemed unthinkable that this could actually happen to the Messiah. Yet, this horrible moment wasn't outside of the sovereign plan of the God of grace. What seemed like the darkest moment in all of human history was, in fact, a bright and shining moment of redemptive love. What seemed like a sad moment of defeat was, in fact, a moment of eternal victory. Psalm 27 looks forward to the cross and captures what happens there, which is recorded in the New Testament. Below are two examples.

Peter's first sermon, in Acts 2:23–24:

> This Jesus, delivered up according to the definite plan and foreknowledge of God, you crucified and killed by the hands of lawless men. God raised him up, loosing the pangs of death, because it was not possible for him to be held by it.

Paul's words about the cross from Colossians 2:14–15:

> Having canceled the written code, with its regulations, that was against us and that stood opposed to us; he took it away, nailing it to the cross. And having disarmed the powers and authorities, he made a public spectacle of them, triumphing over them by the cross. (NIV)

Doesn't Psalm 27 predict exactly what these passages look back to and say about the cross? These words, "When my enemies and my foes attack me, they will stumble and fall," mirror Paul's words, "He made a public spectacle of them, triumphing over them by the cross."

The cross wasn't an unexpected moment outside the plan of God in which Jesus faced temporary defeat. On the contrary, it was the ultimate moment of stumbling for the forces of darkness. In what looked like the enemy's time of triumph, he was actually being dealt his ultimate defeat. From the moment of the fall of Adam and Eve, the enemy was destined to stumble at the cross.

There was no possibility that Jesus would be defeated. Peter makes it clear that the outcome had been determined before the foundations of the earth had been put in place. God had controlled the forces of nature and written the events of human history to bring the promised Messiah, the sacrificial Lamb, the hope of the world, to this point. The hope of the universe rested on this moment. Yet, there was no doubt his moment of suffering would be the universe's moment of victory and freedom. This circumstance of death would be a triumph of eternal life. It was destined to be; it would not be Christ, but the enemy, who would stumble and fall.

Read Psalm 27 and see your suffering Savior. Read Psalm 27 and celebrate your redemption. Read Psalm 27 and remember that in the stumbling of the enemy your life and hope is to be found. Read Psalm 27 and be filled with deep appreciation for sovereign grace.

The enemy stumbled at the cross so that your hope would never stumble and fall. If you have hope in Christ, you have hope that is guaranteed and sure.

Take a Moment

1. Do you live in hope or have you grown weary, bitter, or cynical about something or someone? If so, are you merely settling for survival?
2. What things in life tend to function as your substitutes for the hope that can be found only at the cross?

51 | Functional Blindness

. . . To gaze upon the beauty of the LORD
and to inquire in his temple.
PSALM 27:4

I would like to think
that others are blind,
but I am not.
I would like to think
that I have
clarity of vision,
a penetrating insight
that lights my way.
I am good
at recognizing
the sight problems of others.
I am skilled
at pointing out
the gaps in their vision
and the blind spots
that alter how they
see
and the way they
respond.
I would like to
believe
that I have 20/20 vision,
but the evidence points
to the sad fact that
I don't.
I have the stunning ability
to look around
and not see You.
I see my

busy schedule
tasks to complete
problems to solve
people to see
demands to be met
things to repair
pressures to face
temptations to fight
pleasures to consume
things to build
things to tear down
plans to make
difficulties to survive
huge responsibilities
and short days.
I gaze at my life
every day
and again and again I fail
to see You.
It is a scary
reality,
humbling to admit.
Though this world
is filled with
Your glory,
I exist
so much of the time
glory blind.
In Your love
You created a world
that is a sight and sound
display
of Your magnificent
glory.
No matter from what perspective
we're looking,
no matter what vista
we're taking in,
no matter
where we're standing
and which way
we're gazing,

Your glory is visible
and evident.
Yet, again and again
I fail to see
Your beauty.
So I seek Your
healing
one more time.
Please place Your
powerful hands
on my broken eyes
and give me sight again.
Please place Your
powerful hands
on my wayward heart
and make it seek again.
Don't let me be
so blinded
with me and mine,
that I fail to see
You.
For it's only
when my eyes
see Your
beauty,
and my heart
is filled with Your
glory
that I'll quit
seeking
identity
meaning
satisfaction
purpose
fulfillment
and life,
where it can't be found.
So I would pray
this simple prayer,
"Please touch me by
Your grace
so that there'll never

be a day
where I haven't
somehow
someway
gazed upon
Your beauty."

Take a Moment

1. What clouds your vision of the Lord?
2. List ten specific places where the glory and beauty of the Lord are a visible reminder of his love for you.

52 | Rest

> Be strong, and let your heart take courage;
> wait for the LORD!
>
> PSALM 27:14

Rest:
a faint dream for many
a treasured commodity
in a fallen world,
a thing so needed,
yet so easily interrupted.
The garden was a place of
rest,
no violence in creation
no weed or thorn
no cleft between God and man
no reason to hide
no cause for fear
no need unmet
no grief to face.
Bright sun
pure love
unfettered peace
unstained beauty
man and God
worship and love.
But a voice
interrupted the rest:
strategies of death
words of deceit
actions of rebellion
fingers of blame
expulsion from the garden
judgment and death
rest interrupted
rest shattered.
So we wait for the Lord.
His grace strengthens
His presence comforts

His promises assure
His power activates
His rule guarantees
that someday rest,
real rest
pure rest
eternal rest
will reign once more.
No violence in creation
no weed or thorn
no cleft between God and man
no reason to hide
no cause for fear
no need unmet
no grief to face
between God and man.
Yes, rest, true rest
will live again
and last forever.
So we wait for the Lord
to restore us to that place.
Bright Son
pure love
unfettered peace
unstained beauty
God and man
together forever.
Until that day,
with hearts
that are strong
and hope
that is undimmed
and joy
that embraces the future,
We wait for the Lord.

Take a Moment

1. What things in life tend to interrupt your rest in the Lord?
2. What present graces is God calling you to celebrate as you wait for that final rest?